BAREFOOT CONQUISTADOR

1
PTA
IV CENTENARIO DE
FLORIDA
CABEZA
DE VACA
CORREOS
ESPAÑA
F.N.M.T.

BAREFOOT CONQUISTADOR

CABEZA DE VACA

AND

THE STRUGGLE

FOR NATIVE AMERICAN RIGHTS

DIANA CHILDRESS

TWENTY-FIRST CENTURY BOOKS · MINNEAPOLIS

For Marcia, editor extraordinaire, with thanks

Page 2: This portrait on a Spanish stamp issued October 12, 1960, is part of a series of eight stamps celebrating the fourth centennial of Spain's discovery of Florida. The portrait is not based on any contemporary portrait, as there is none.

Twenty-First Century Books
A division of Lerner Publishing Group, Inc.
241 First Avenue North
Minneapolis, MN 55401 U.S.A.

Website address: www.lernerbooks.com

Library of Congress Cataloging-in-Publication Data

Childress, Diana.
    Barefoot conquistador : Cabeza de Vaca and the struggle for
    Native American rights / by Diana Childress.
        p. cm.
    Includes bibliographical references and index.
    ISBN 978–0–8225–7517–7 (lib. bdg. : alk. paper)
    1. Núñez Cabeza de Vaca, Alvar, 16th cent. 2. Explorers—
America—Biography. 3. Explorers—Spain—Biography. 4.
America—Discovery and exploration—Spanish. 5. Indians,
Treatment of—America—History. 6. Indians—First contact with
Europeans. I. Title.
E125.N9C47 2008
970.01'6092—dc22   2007022059

Manufactured in the United States of America
1 2 3 4 5 6 – BP – 13 12 11 10 09 08

Contents

ROLOGUE

SHIPWRECKED

Clouds hung heavy over the bay, and waves chopped the November sea into gray peaks. But the forty-nine Europeans camped on the beach felt ready to resume their grueling journey.

In late September 1528, the men had all crowded into a hand-built open boat the length of two midsize cars to row and sail their way westward from the Florida Panhandle to the coast of Mexico. For six weeks, sun and rain beat down on them and Native American arrows often kept them from replenishing food and freshwater. Supplies grew so low that each man's daily ration was half a handful of dried corn. Then, in early November, a storm blew the rickety craft ashore on a Texas island where welcoming Indians gave them fish and roots to eat.

Although still weak, the men were now determined to resume their voyage to Spanish settlements in Mexico. To keep their tattered clothing dry, they stripped down and stowed it safely aboard while wading out to set the vessel afloat. Still undressed, they piled in and rowed out into the rough water. A huge great wave broke over them. Stunned by the icy deluge, the rowers dropped their oars to grab the sides of the lurching boat. A larger wave seized the small vessel and flipped it over.

Three men did not let go and drowned under the capsized craft. The rest scrambled back to land, hauling their lifeless companions with them, all "naked as we had been born," their leader, Álvar Núñez Cabeza de Vaca, wrote later.

Biting north winds buffeted the scrawny men, their skin shrunk taut against their bones. They raked the fires they had just recently put out and dragged driftwood to the glowing coals. Flames sprouted and licked at the wood. In tears, the men knelt to beg God for mercy and forgiveness for their sins. No one wept just for himself, Cabeza de Vaca said, but for everyone, for they all shared the same fate.

As leader of the small band, Cabeza de Vaca had to decide what to do next. The men had set sail from Spain seventeen months earlier. They were then proud conquerors with ambitious plans to explore, and settle an area of North America they knew little about. They had survived hurricanes and the loss of their ships, escaped numerous attacks, and endured fevers and hunger. Now everything they had—their clothing, their scant food supplies, their weapons, their trinkets to trade with Indians, and their means of escape—lay scattered at the bottom of the bay. Cabeza de Vaca realized that the tough, swaggering men-at-arms would have to trust in the care and kindness of others—in this case, the native peoples they had until this time treated as enemies or servants. It was their only hope.

What Cabeza de Vaca learned that day informed the rest of his life. Never again would he look on Native Americans in the way most Europeans did—as threatening obstacles to overcome or useful labor to enslave. For stripped of all the trappings of European civilization, he recognized what he and they had in common—their shared humanity.

This experience marked the beginning of Cabeza de Vaca's deeper understanding of Native American culture and humanity, his concern for the welfare of native peoples, and his struggle to bring them liberty and justice in a time of unbridled greed, self-interest, and cruelty. The story of his two remarkable expeditions in North and South America is the story of one Spaniard who stands out as a shining light in the dark world of Spain's conquest of the Americas.

Cabeza de Vaca's account of his travels through Texas and Mexico, called the Relación *(The Account), was published in 1542. A second, slightly revised version came out in 1555. Known as* Naufragios *(Shipwrecks), it also included* Comentarios *written by his secretary, Pedro Hernández, about the later expedition to South America. This is the title page from the 1555* Naufragios. *This edition is the basis for most translations of Cabeza de Vaca's story of his adventures.*

CABALLERO OF JEREZ

Álvar Núñez Cabeza de Vaca was born in Jerez de la Frontera, Spain, around 1488 into a world long dominated by war and conquest. More than seven centuries earlier, Islamic warriors from North Africa had defeated and slain the Christian ruler of Spain, not far from Cabeza de Vaca's birthplace. The Islamic invaders soon conquered most of modern-day Spain and Portugal. The Christians retreated north and then began to fight back. They called their long struggle to regain their lost lands *La Reconquista*—"The Reconquest."

According to a legend, the unusual name Cabeza de Vaca, which means "Head of a Cow," came about during this struggle. A shepherd, the story goes, showed a Christian army the way to cross a strategic mountain pass by marking it with a cow's skull. After surprising and defeating the Islamic army on the other side of the mountains, the Christian king made the shepherd a knight and gave him the name Cabeza de Vaca. This myth, however, has no historic basis, and there is no evidence Cabeza de Vaca ever heard it. But his ancestors did play a role in the Reconquista.

As a member of the middle tier of Spanish nobility—a class known as caballeros for the horses (*caballos*) they rode in battle—Álvar descended from a long line of warriors. Álvar's mother, Doña Teresa Cabeza de Vaca, named him for her great-grandfather, who in the early 1400s had led a victorious sea battle south of Spain in the Straits of Gibraltar. His father's father, Pedro de Vera, not only fought in the Reconquista but in the 1480s led the conquest of Grand Canary Island off the coast of Morocco in North Africa.

The rulers of Spain, Queen Isabella and King Ferdinand, were eager to claim the Canary Islands in order to expand Spanish trade with Africa. The islands were then inhabited by herders and farmers who had migrated from Africa. They had no iron tools or weapons and worshipped the sun, moon, and other natural forces. When the Spanish came, the Canarians hid out in the mountains and shoved boulders down on their attackers. To starve them into submission, Pedro de Vera burned their crops and killed their livestock.

A chronicle from the time, however, describes Pedro de Vera as a "*cavallero esforçado*" (hardy knight) who defeated the Canarian chieftain in combat and led a brilliant amphibious assault on the rocky west coast of the island. On the day that the islanders surrendered and agreed to accept Spanish rule and the Christian religion, the chronicle says an eclipse hid the sun and a great storm blew wind and rain across the island. Álvar, his three sisters, and three younger brothers grew up hearing such romantic stories about their illustrious ancestors.

Young Álvar saw people from the Canary Islands in Jerez, for his grandfather sent Canarians captured in the war to be sold as slaves in Spain. Queen Isabella and King Ferdinand,

This nineteenth-century painting by Carlos Luis Ribera y Fieve portrays the Moors (Islamic African conquerors of Spain) surrendering Granada to King Ferdinand and Queen Isabella in 1492. This event brought an end to the long struggle by Christian rulers of Spain to regain their land from the Moors, who had conquered the Iberian Peninsula (Spain and Portugal) in the early 700s.

however, declared it illegal to enslave baptized Christians and forced Vera to repay those who bought his slaves. Yet in spite of royal efforts to discourage enslavement, many Canarians were forced to labor on plantations on the islands or brought against their will to Spain to work as domestic servants. Some may have worked in Álvar's boyhood home.

By the time of Álvar's birth, the only part of Spain still under Islamic rule was the kingdom of Granada. Cabeza de Vaca's hometown lay close to the border of this Islamic kingdom. As a child, Álvar would have seen one thousand horsemen and foot soldiers gather in Jerez to prepare for the final assault on Granada. Pedro de Vera played a leading role in the campaign. In January 1492, the Muslims were defeated, and Spanish Christians celebrated the end of the Reconquista.

Historians know little about Álvar's beginnings other than

that he belonged to a respected family. His father, Francisco de Vera, sat on the city council of Jerez, not joining his father and older brothers in the Canaries. Perhaps he was looking after family affairs back home. After Álvar's paternal grandfather returned to Jerez, he also served on the city council.

When Álvar was about fifteen, he left home to become a page in the household of the Duke of Medina Sidonia. He did not go far, as the duke's many estates, like Jerez itself, lay in Cadiz Province in southeastern Spain. Service in the households of the upper nobility was the principal source of higher education for young caballeros not planning to have a career in the Roman Catholic Church. As a page, Álvar trained to fight on horseback, learned proper etiquette, and attended members of the duke's family. Some years later, one of Álvar's brothers and a cousin joined him on the duke's payroll.

In 1511, when he was in his early twenties, Cabeza de Vaca had his first taste of military life. King Ferdinand had requested the duke's help in defending Spanish-held lands in Italy from French attack. After sailing to Naples, Cabeza de Vaca marched north with Spanish forces to besiege the French at Bologna in northern Italy. The French, however, overcame the Spanish in battle and chased them eastward to Ravenna. There the Spaniards suffered a bloody rout. An estimated twenty thousand men died in the battle, with equal numbers lost on each side. So many French soldiers were killed that they too retreated and gave up their conquest of northern Italy.

Cabeza de Vaca was among the many wounded, *"muy destroçado"* (very beaten up) a companion later said. But he distinguished himself in battle, for after the Spanish later returned to Naples and Cabeza de Vaca recovered from his wounds, he was promoted and posted as a lieutenant in the

Italian city of Gaeta.

Cabeza de Vaca returned to the duke's service in Spain in 1513. Six years later, he had become his steward, a kind of personal assistant entrusted with family business.

Around this time, Cabeza de Vaca married Maria Marmolejo. Little is known about his marriage, other than that the Marmolejo family were *conversos*—Jews who had converted to Roman Catholicism. Many Jews in Spain converted to Christianity during the late 1300s and early 1400s, when there was widespread anti-Jewish violence in Spain, and later in 1492, when Queen Isabella and King Ferdinand gave Jews the choice of converting to Christianity or leaving the country. Conversos often held important positions at court and married Christian nobles.

In 1520 Cabeza de Vaca saw military action again, this time in Spain. The new, twenty-year-old Spanish king, Charles I, had just inherited from his grandfather the right to rule the Holy Roman Empire, a large federation of German and Italian

On May 30, 1516, Charles I (right) inherited his grandfather Ferdinand's realm, which included regions in Spain and southern Italy. Three years later, Charles also became the Holy Roman Emperor, Charles V, making him the most powerful monarch in Europe. During his reign, Spain's conquests in the Americas added to Spanish wealth and prestige.

territories. When Charles left Spain to claim his new title, many cities in northern and central Spain rebelled against him, for they were afraid that, as Holy Roman Emperor, Charles would get embroiled in costly faraway wars. The noble families of southern Spain, however, backed the new king. As one of the Duke of Medina Sidonia's caballeros, Cabeza de Vaca helped rescue the royal fortress in Seville from the rebel faction. After Seville was secured, Cabeza de Vaca was entrusted with guarding one of the city gates.

The duke then sent Cabeza de Vaca north to the royal court at Valladolid to confer with royalist leaders. He took part in two other battles before the revolt was finally suppressed. Perhaps because he was already in northern Castile, Cabeza de Vaca also saw action in Navarre, a kingdom on the Spanish border that the French were trying to annex.

Cabeza de Vaca was now moving in the highest circles of Spanish power as the Duke of Medina Sidonia's representative at the royal court. In 1524 he described himself with some pride as employed by "the illustrious and very magnificent lord the duke of Medina Sidonia." At some point during the next three years, however, Cabeza de Vaca left the duke's service to become an official of the king. It was a career move that sent him in a completely new direction.

CONQUERING
THE NEW WORLD

As Cabeza de Vaca was growing up, Spain was vying with Portugal to find a new sea route to eastern Asia and its rich markets of spices, silks, carpets, and gems. The navigator Christopher Columbus tried to reach Asia by sailing west from the Canary Islands in 1492, but he stumbled on the Americas instead. During Cabeza de Vaca's childhood, the significance of Columbus's discoveries gradually dawned on Europeans. By 1500 the explorer Amerigo Vespucci was certain that what lay across the Atlantic was not Asia but a "New World." Spaniards, however, continued to call the islands and continents the Indies, just as they referred to all the many different peoples who lived there as Indians.

Exciting reports of new sources of wealth there lured many young men to join expeditions to explore and conquer these lands. Most of them were artisans or hidalgos—members of the lowest rung on the ladder of nobility. These

This lithograph, based on a painting by a nineteenth-century Portuguese artist, Ricardo Bolaca, shows Christopher Columbus (center with hand raised) *as he sets sail in 1492 in an attempt to discover a new route to India and the Far East by sailing westward from Europe.*

adventurers were not sailing out into the unknown just to see or plunder what was there. They wanted to expand Spanish territory. Like Cabeza de Vaca's grandfather Pedro de Vera, they were *conquistadores* ("conquerors," or as these Spanish conquerors are called in English, conquistadors).

Their motives were mixed. Like the warriors of the Reconquista, they wished to spread Christianity, but they also hoped to find gold and silver, fertile lands suitable for growing cash crops and raising livestock, and people willing to work in the mines or fields. As the conquistador Bernal Díaz del Castillo wrote, they fought "in the service of God and of His Majesty, and to give light to those who sat in darkness— and also to acquire wealth which most men covet."

During his travels around Spain on the duke's business, Cabeza de Vaca no doubt crossed paths with a number of conquistadors and certainly heard news of their explorations and conquests. At some point, in Toledo in 1525 or in Seville or Granada the following year, he met Pánfilo de Narváez. This tall, fat, one-eyed conquistador with his flaming red hair and beard, ruddy face, and booming voice—which sounded, one chronicler says, like it came from a deep cave—must have made a vivid impression on Cabeza de Vaca.

Born to an hidalgo family around 1478 near Valladolid in northern Spain, Narváez—like most conquistadors—had started young. In his early twenties, he sailed to Hispaniola, the Caribbean island that is today shared by Haiti and the Dominican Republic. There he joined expeditions to Jamaica and Cuba, where he won a reputation for courage and fighting skill. In Cuba, Narváez was rewarded for his military service with an *encomienda*—a group of local villages from which he could collect tribute and labor.

In 1519 the governor of Cuba, Diego de Velázquez, sent one of his captains, Hernán Cortés, to explore the coast of Mexico for a good port to use as a staging area for an *entrada* (literally "entry"), meaning an armed expedition for conquest or plunder. Some months later came news of a ship loaded with gold that had stopped briefly in Cuba without reporting to the authorities. Suspecting a mutiny, Velázquez sent Narváez to Mexico to investigate.

Narváez sailed with eighteen ships, eight hundred soldiers, and eighty horses to the vicinity of modern Veracruz, Mexico. There he learned that Cortés, having discovered the vast wealth of the Aztec Empire, had ignored Velázquez's orders and seized the opportunity to make an entrada of his own. The mysterious ship that stopped in Cuba had been loaded with gifts from the Aztec emperor Moctezuma. It had then sailed on to Spain, where Cortés hoped the rich treasure would influence the king to name him governor of the territory he hoped to conquer.

Cortés, meanwhile, had marched inland to the Aztec capital in what is now Mexico City. Hearing of Narváez's arrival, Cortés marched his men back to the coast. Catching Narváez by surprise, he defeated him in an attack that left Narváez blind in one eye. After imprisoning Narváez, Cortés marched back to the Aztec capital, his troops now reinforced with Narváez's men. One of the men who had come with Narváez was infected with smallpox. Aided by the additional forces and the smallpox germs—the Aztecs had no resistance to the disease—Cortés conquered the Aztec Empire.

Smallpox devastated the Aztecs after it was introduced by one of Narváez's men. This reproduction of an Aztec drawing portrays shroud-covered and dying Aztecs during the epidemic of 1538.

After several years of living "shackled and in chains," Narváez somehow gained his freedom. He returned to Spain to denounce Cortés as "a man without truth," who was "treacherous and tyrannical and ungrateful to his king." But Narváez was not one to wallow in vindictiveness. What he wanted more than anything else was the chance to lead his own expedition of conquest. When he met Cabeza de Vaca, Narváez had his one good eye set on North America, where rumor suggested that another wealthy empire, perhaps even richer than the Aztec Empire, might be found. For over a year, Narváez traveled with the court around Spain, petitioning the king to name him *adelantado*—leader of an expedition to explore, conquer, and settle a specific area.

A fellow conquistador, Gonzalo Fernández de Oviedo, tried to talk Narváez out of the idea. Like Narváez, Oviedo was in his late forties. He had retired from military life to pursue the quieter career of writing the history of the Spanish conquest of the Indies for the king. He advised Narváez, "as a friend, to take up a calmer life at home in the company of his wife and children." But Narváez was not ready to give up his dream.

Two sources describe Narváez as agreeable and a good conversationalist. Perhaps he was also a persuasive recruiter. It is possible that Cabeza de Vaca, seeing the energy and drive of this man some ten years older than himself, was inspired to join his new venture.

But it is also possible that Cabeza de Vaca joined Narváez's expedition because the royal court and the Council of the Indies, which advised the king on American policy, wanted him there. Cabeza de Vaca had military experience and knew something of diplomacy and administration. He could be trusted to act as the eyes and ears of the king. He was also a man with sufficient authority to ensure that

Narváez fulfilled the obligations of his contract and did not take more than his share of the wealth the expedition would find, a man who could stand up to Narváez if necessary. Perhaps he signed on because the king requested it.

No letters, diaries, or memoirs reveal what Cabeza de Vaca was thinking. He was not a youthful, ambitious hidalgo like the men typically drawn to the Indies. It was a major gamble for a man of his age and standing.

On December, 11, 1526, Pánfilo de Narváez received a grant to lead an expedition to Río de las Palmas and Cape Florida, a huge area that stretched along the Gulf of Mexico from what is now northern Mexico to the Florida Peninsula. Unaware of the distance across the North American continent at that latitude, the Spanish court also gave Narváez permission to conquer inland from "one sea to the other," that is from the Gulf Coast as far as the Pacific Ocean—all the way from Florida to California. Álvar Núñez Cabeza de Vaca was named treasurer, the highest-ranking royal official on the expedition.

PREPARING FOR
THE ENTRADA

During the year that Narváez petitioned the king, the royal court was drafting new procedures in response to complaints brought against Diego de Velázquez, Cortés, and other conquistadors concerning their treatment of the Indians. According to Spanish laws, conquistadors were supposed to give protection, Christian instruction, and wages to Native Americans in exchange for their labor, but most conquistadors treated Indians as slaves or enemies. Bartolomé de las Casas, a conquistador turned priest, was among the voices speaking out against this abuse.

In November 1526, new laws governing conquests became the basis for all future contracts. These new laws required that priests accompany each expedition and decide on the justice of waging war on native peoples. Military force could be used only if native peoples refused to submit to Spanish rule. The laws called for continuing a practice begun in 1513: when arriving in a new territory, the Spanish conquering expedition was to read to the inhabitants a document known as the *requerimiento*—"the ultimatum."

The requerimiento proclaimed that the lands the indigenous people lived on had been allotted to the Spanish monarch by the pope (the leader of the Roman Catholic Church)—defined as "admirable great father and governor of men." This claim referred to the Treaty of Tordesillas between Spain and Portugal, which the pope had approved in 1494. This agreement gave Spain the exclusive right to conquer and settle non-Christian lands west of a north-south line 370 leagues (about 1,270 miles) west of the Cape Verde Islands in the South Atlantic Ocean off Africa. Portugal received the right to lands east of the line.

The requerimiento alleged that other Native Americans, hearing this news, had at once agreed to welcome the priests

This twentieth-century painting by Antonio Menendez shows the negotiations that led to the 1494 Treaty of Tordesillas, which divided non-Christian lands outside of Europe between Portugal and Spain.

accompanying the conquistadors, learn about Christianity, and become Christian subjects of Spain. It offered them time to deliberate before choosing to acknowledge the church as ruler of the whole world and the Spanish king as their king.

If they received the priests and listened to their teachings, the proclamation promised, native peoples would be allowed to keep their wives, children, and lands and live as freemen without servitude. They did not need to convert to Christianity if they did not wish to do so.

But if they refused, the requerimiento warned:

> We shall powerfully enter into your country, and shall make war against you in all ways and manners that we can . . . ; we shall take you and your wives and your children, and shall make slaves of them . . . ; and we shall take away your goods, and shall do you all the mischief and damage that we can, as to vassals who do not obey, and refuse to accept their lord, and resist and contradict him; and we protest that the deaths and losses that shall accrue from this are your fault.

Basically the message was: Accept King Charles as your sovereign, and we will treat you well. Refuse and we will make war on you and make you our slaves. It did not require native peoples to become Christians but did insist that they acknowledge the superiority of the Christian religion and submit to Spanish rule.

In December the court issued Narváez a contract that fills seven double-columned pages in a modern edition. It granted Narváez permission to "discover, explore, and settle" the vast area assigned to him. He was to establish two towns and three fortresses, taking with him at least one hundred men to live in each town, all at his own expense.

Much of the contract concerned legal and commercial details of the colony, such as taxes, Narváez's salary and titles, and how much land members of the expedition should receive. It granted Narváez's request for permission to enslave rebellious native peoples and to trade in slaves, but it required him to take clergy with him and to treat peaceable Indians humanely, "as free men and not as slaves."

The court named three royal officials to accompany Narváez and look after the king's financial interests. Like Cabeza de Vaca, the other two seem not to have had previous experience in the Indies. Each received a contract listing his duties. As treasurer, Cabeza de Vaca was responsible for all royal revenues. One-fifth of all the wealth accumulated on the expedition belonged to the king. He was also obliged to report to the Council of the Indies "extensively and particularly of every matter" concerning the progress of the conquest. The comptroller, Alonso Enríquez, was to keep track of expenditures made from the royal income, such as the salaries of the officials and costs incurred in establishing a government in the new colony. And Diego de Solís, as tax agent and inspector, was to collect and deliver to the treasurer all taxes and oversee merchandise and property in the colony. Each officer had one key to a chest with three locks in which all the king's money was to be kept, and each was urged to work with the others.

Religious officials of the Council of the Indies appointed five Franciscan friars (members of a Christian religious group that carries out the teachings of Saint Francis of Assisi) to accompany the expedition. Juan Suárez, the leader of the group, and one other friar had been to Mexico in 1524.

With six months to prepare for the journey, Narváez got busy. He purchased five caravels (small three-masted ships), chose pilots and seamen to sail them, appointed captains to recruit men-at-arms and artisans for the expedition, and arranged for a lengthy absence from Spain by assigning someone to oversee his affairs while he was gone.

Like the others, Cabeza de Vaca appointed his wife or a family member to take care of any business that came up. Cabeza de Vaca also raised money to leave a deposit of two thousand gold ducats as security that he would carry out his duties. Two thousand ducats was a large sum, equal to five and a half times the annual salary he was to receive as treasurer. More money went to buy weapons and armor, boots and clothing, and other necessities for the journey.

Much of the work assembling materials and crew took place in Seville. Spread out on the left bank of the Guadalquivir River, about sixty miles from the Atlantic Ocean, Seville was the largest city in Spain. It was still circled by old walls built by Muslims before Christian forces captured the city in the 1200s. But after being made the official port of entry and departure for ships going to America in 1503, suburbs had spread out beyond the walls and even across the river over a pontoon bridge north of town.

The city bustled with maritime activity. The captains of Narváez's ships scouted for crew members among seamen waiting for jobs on stone steps leading up to Seville's Gothic cathedral. In booths nearby, notaries prepared contracts of employment and other legal papers for overseas ventures.

Cabeza de Vaca also went to Seville to prepare for his voyage. He and the other royal officials presented their instructions at the House of Trade, the government agency that

This 1594 engraving by Theodor de Bry depicts the bustling port of Seville, Spain, much as it would have looked to Cabeza de Vaca in the 1520s.

controlled all commerce with the Indies. Here they were briefed about their assignments and the geography of the region. A map published in 1527 shows the kind of information Cabeza de Vaca received. It sketches a reasonably accurate picture of the coastline of the Gulf of Mexico and names a number of rivers but provides few geographical details to differentiate one river from another. Inland north and west of the Gulf, the map is marked "the lands that Narváez is now going to settle."

The Pacific coast of this map ends abruptly in southern Mexico. In 1527 Spanish ships had explored the west coast of Mexico only as far north as Cabo Corrientes, a cape that juts out from the coast almost due west from Mexico City. One of the goals of the Narvácz cxpcdition was to extend Spanish knowledge of the west coast of North America.

Besides maps, Cabeza de Vaca studied reports of earlier

explorers. Juan Ponce de León had discovered the Florida Peninsula fourteen years earlier, and the governor of Jamaica had also financed several explorations along the coast. His men reported that Florida is not an island (as Ponce de León thought) and that "along a lengthy, roundabout course," it is connected to Mexico.

The reports also noted that in 1521, Ponce de León had returned to Florida with more than two hundred soldiers and friars in four ships well stocked with farm animals, tools, and seeds to start a colony. But hostile natives prevented them from building their settlement. In his chronicle of the event, the historian Oviedo described the Florida Indians as "very tough and very savage and warlike and fierce and incapable of being tamed." The failed expedition retreated to Cuba, where Ponce de León died from an arrow wound.

Accounts of Río de las Palmas were not much more hopeful. Named for the palm trees lining its banks, Río de las Palmas is the Mexican river called Soto la Marina, which empties into the Gulf of Mexico about 150 miles south of the United States–Mexico border. Spaniards who landed there described a thinly populated wilderness of cactus and small, thorny mesquite trees growing near creeks and rivers. They saw no farmland or villages or sign of any kind of wealth.

The only optimistic note in the information Narváez and Cabeza de Vaca received came from a Spanish outpost on the Pánuco River, 110 miles south of Río de las Palmas. Spaniards there had traded with natives for large nuggets of gold. Apparently, somewhere farther inland there were mines— and perhaps even a civilization as rich as the Aztec Empire.

Sometime in June of 1527, Narváez, Cabeza de Vaca, and about six hundred men, at least ten with their wives and at least two with their African slaves, boarded the five ships anchored along the broad sandy beach below the walls of Seville. The trip downriver took about a week, for the ships had to navigate past several shallow areas in the river, some only two feet deep at low tide. At Sanlúcar de Barrameda, the small fleet had to wait again for the right wind and tide to sail over a sandbar at the mouth of the Guadalquivir.

Cabeza de Vaca's cousin, Pedro Estopiñan, and quite likely his wife, Maria Marmolejo Cabeza de Vaca, and other family members took the ten-mile journey from Jerez to wish their adventurous kinsman *buen viaje* (good voyage). As exciting as the anticipation of traveling to a New World was, such good-byes must have been difficult. Sea journeys were perilous. One Spaniard commented that it was madness to put one's life and fortune "three or four fingers away from death, which is the thickness of a ship's planking." Other dangers lurked beyond the ocean. Indian arrows, tropical diseases, and starvation claimed many conquistadors' lives. The odds of returning from the Indies were not high.

At last, on June 27, 1527, trusting in themselves and God, the Narváez expedition sailed out into the Atlantic. We know the date because ten years later, when Cabeza de Vaca wrote his account of the voyage for King Charles, he opened his story on that day.

ACROSS THE ATLANTIC
TO THE INDIES

By 1527 travel across the Atlantic from Spain to the Indies was reasonably predictable. Three and a half decades of transatlantic travel had established the best times and routes for crossings. A June departure was ideal, for it was after the winter storms in Europe ended, and the five- or six-week journey would get them to the Caribbean before the hurricane season started there.

For the first week or ten days after leaving the coast of Spain, the ships sailed southwest to the Canary Islands. Here passengers took a brief break ashore while the crew stocked up on freshwater and firewood. For Cabeza de Vaca, the islands must have evoked memories of his grandfather and the stories of conquest he heard as a child. Now at nearly forty years of age, he was at last stepping into his

Narváez and his crew sailed toward the Americas in five caravels. This woodcut of a similar three-masted caravel is from an illustrated edition of a letter by Christopher Columbus published in 1493.

grandfather's shoes as a conqueror of new lands and people for Spain and the Catholic faith. Most likely he felt proud to be part of such a noble venture.

From the Canaries, the Narváez fleet rode the trade winds westward for about a month to Hispaniola, then the center of Spanish rule in the Americas. The ships arrived in the port of Santo Domingo in mid-August. While Narváez purchased horses and other supplies, including a sixth ship, many of the men had second thoughts about going with him to Florida. In his account, Cabeza de Vaca reports that "more than 140 men of our army left us, wishing to remain as a result of the proposals and promises they had received from the people of the country."

Cabeza de Vaca does not say what kind of attractive offers they received. Perhaps some men jumped ship to join a different expedition, such as one about to leave for Yucatán. Others might have found jobs managing sugar plantations or overseeing mine workers, more secure work than exploration and conquest.

It is also possible that so many men—almost a quarter of the force—abandoned the venture because they mistrusted or disliked its leader. The affable man who persuaded them to join his expedition with upbeat speeches may have revealed a harsher side on the long journey in the close confines of a crowded ship. Whatever the reason, such a large loss of manpower must have cast a shadow over the enterprise.

After six weeks on Hispaniola, Narváez sailed with his reduced forces to Cuba for more men, arms, and horses. The fleet landed at Santiago on the eastern end of the island, where a colonist Narváez knew from his time in Cuba offered to sell him supplies that he had in the town of Trinidad, about three hundred miles away along the low, swampy south coast of the island. Narváez sent Cabeza de Vaca with two ships to collect the provisions.

As Cabeza de Vaca was ashore getting the supplies loaded into boats to bring to the ships, a great hurricane struck. "All the houses and churches came crashing down," Cabeza de Vaca wrote years later, the memory still vivid in his mind. "We had to lock arms and walk seven or eight men together to prevent the wind from carrying us off. It was no less dangerous under the trees than among the houses, since they were also being blown down and we were in danger of being killed underneath them."

Both ships waiting near the shore were torn from their anchors, blown for miles down the coast, and dashed against

Spanish explorers in the Indies often experienced violent storms that the Tainos (early inhabitants of the Caribbean) called hurakan. This 1594 engraving by de Bry depicts a hurricane that occurred during Columbus's second voyage to the Americas in 1494. Although de Bry, who was from the Netherlands, never left Europe, he based his illustrations on descriptions and original works from explorers.

rocks. Sixty men and twenty horses aboard the ships drowned. The next day, Cabeza de Vaca found a rowboat from one of the ships atop trees a mile inland, while along the beach he saw only a cape and a quilt ripped to pieces, some lids of crates, and two bodies so battered that no one could identify them.

Narváez and the four other ships had found shelter in time and arrived November 5 to find Cabeza de Vaca and thirty other survivors pinched with hunger. No one was eager to start out for the mainland that late in the year. Fearing more rough weather, the flotilla sailed to a better port farther west on Cienfuegos Bay and remained there until February 1528. Narváez, meanwhile, purchased a brigantine—a smaller, two-masted sailing ship—and hired a pilot who claimed familiarity with the Gulf Coast between Río de las Palmas and Florida.

On February 22, the four caravels and one brigantine carrying four hundred men and eighty horses set sail. But the going was rough. First, the ships ran aground on a sandbar and were stuck for two weeks until a squall blew them free. More storms prevented them from reaching Havana on the north shore of the island where a sixth ship, with fifty-two men, twelve horses, and food for the new settlement, waited to join them. The gale blew them north into the Gulf of Mexico.

In early April, the storm-tossed fleet sighted land at last. Sailing south along the coast, they came to a bay with a small settlement. The comptroller met with some people living on an island in the bay and returned to the ships with fish and venison. After more than a month at sea, fresh food must have been welcome.

When Cabeza de Vaca and some of the other Spaniards went ashore the next day, however, they found the village deserted. During the night, the inhabitants had fled in their canoes. As the men explored the houses, one of which was large enough to hold three hundred people, they found a gold rattle among the fishing nets. Everyone's hopes soared. Here might be an area worth conquering.

The next day, Narváez took formal possession of the land in the name of King Charles. Cabeza de Vaca does not mention any reading of the requerimiento—there were no Native Americans present to hear it anyway—but a ceremony took place in which the royal officials presented their credentials to Narváez, the governor, and a flag was raised in the king's name. Then the rest of the men disembarked to set up a military camp. Thirty-eight horses had died on the voyage. The forty-two surviving horses, weak and thin from the long journey, limped ashore to graze.

A group of the local inhabitants returned the next day. Having no interpreter on the expedition, the Spaniards understood nothing they said. But their threatening gestures made it clear that they wanted the Spaniards to leave. The native people then went away peacefully.

The Spaniards now had to figure out where they were. After a brief overland hike to scout the territory, Narváez ordered the brigantine to sail down the coast to look for Río de las Palmas, where Narváez hoped to establish his first town. The pilot seems to have had no idea how far they were from their goal. Historians believe that the expedition made landfall on the western coast of the Florida Peninsula, just north of the entrance to Tampa Bay. Río de las Palmas was at the opposite end of Narváez's assigned lands, more than one thousand miles to the west.

It is not clear why the pilot confused the west coast of Florida with the east coast of Mexico. Perhaps overcast weather made it difficult at first to determine directions, although the ship's compass should have set them straight. Some historians think that the pilot had some other port, not the mouth of Río de las Palmas, in mind.

Narváez, at any rate, sent the brigantine southward, telling the men that if they did not find the port, to sail back to Cuba to pick up more supplies and the ship waiting in Havana. The two vessels were then to return to look for the rest of the expedition.

Meanwhile, Cabeza de Vaca, the other royal officials, and about fifty men went with Narváez to explore inland. Coming upon a few people, they showed them some dried corn in hopes of replenishing their food supplies. The people took them to a village at the end of a bay where young cornstalks grew in a field. The village itself was deserted. Many of the local inhabitants abandoned their homes as news of the Spanish arrival spread. They likely knew a fair amount about Europeans and did not wish to risk meeting them. Even if no ships had made landfall in that area before, people living there would have heard from trading partners about slavers carrying people away in their ships.

If the lack of ripe corn was a disappointment, the Spaniards found other things in the village both ominous and hopeful. Inside a large number of wooden boxes that looked as if they had come from Spain, they discovered corpses covered in painted deerskins. Friar Suárez decided

De Bry based this engraving on a watercolor by French artist Jacques Le Moyne, who traveled to Florida with a French expedition in 1564. The picture shows French settlers seeking food from Native Americans. It shows indigenous housing, styles of dress, methods of transportation, and flora and fauna, such as palmettos and crocodiles.

that the crates held religious significance to the Indians and ordered them destroyed, so the Spaniards burned them and the corpses. It seems not to have occurred to them at the time that the bodies might be those of Europeans.

The Spaniards also saw feather headdresses that reminded them of the Aztec treasures Cortés had sent to Spain, as well as linen cloth and samples of gold. Using signs, the Spaniards asked the source of these treasures. They interpreted the Indians' response to mean that "very far away there was a province called Apalache in which there was a great deal of gold."

Yet everything they were looking at probably came from a Spanish shipwreck, not an unknown wealthy civilization somewhere inland. The gold and the headdresses were likely stolen Aztec treasures, and the cloth was probably Spanish.

Perhaps the excitement of finding gold kept them from thinking things through. They had come to North America with the hope and expectation of locating new sources of precious metals. The Indians were now holding gold nuggets, pointing north, and saying "Apalache." The only logical thing to do was go there, taking some Indians with them as guides. After traveling about thirty miles farther to another deserted village for a good supply of ripe corn, the Spaniards returned to where the main group was waiting with the ships to tell them what they had learned.

On the first of May, Narváez called a meeting of the royal officials, Friar Suárez, a notary, and the captain of one of the ships. He proposed to take most of the men and march inland parallel to the coast while the ships followed by sea. He argued this was the best way to find the harbor at Río de las Palmas, which the pilot had assured him was not far away. He asked for their opinions.

Cabeza de Vaca disagreed. "I replied that it seemed to me in no way advisable to leave the ships until they were in a safe, occupied port." He pointed out the disadvantages of being unable to make themselves understood to the Native Americans, of not knowing what kind of land or people to expect, and of being low on food.

"In my opinion," he concluded, "we should go back on ship and sail in search of a land and harbor better adapted to settlement, since the country we had seen was the poorest and most desolate ever found in those parts." According to Oviedo's account of the expedition, Cabeza de Vaca further advised Narváez to await the return of the brigantine and the supplies from Havana before starting any overland journey.

Friar Suárez sided with Narváez and reminded everyone of the terrible weather that had battered them at sea. The other officials agreed with him. Cabeza de Vaca, however, felt so strongly that Narváez was making a serious mistake that he repeated his request several times. Adding to the tension, Cabeza de Vaca made sure that the notary—who was the only one present to agree with him—wrote down everything he said. It was a dramatic confrontation. The seasoned conquistador surely resented a rookie who knew nothing of the Indies trying to interfere with his plans. Cabeza de Vaca stood firm. It was his duty as the king's principal representative to speak his mind.

Narváez's patience grew thin. Cabeza de Vaca had no authority to make these demands, he declared. He ordered the company to prepare to march inland, and taunting Cabeza de Vaca with being afraid, he appointed him to take charge of the ships and to establish a settlement when they reached Río de las Palmas. Cabeza de Vaca refused.

Now it was Narváez's turn to beg. That afternoon as the men prepared to leave, he urged Cabeza de Vaca to take charge of the ships, "saying that it seemed to him that he could trust no one else." But Cabeza de Vaca could not easily brush aside the slap to his honor. He was certain, Cabeza de Vaca responded, that the overland trek was so poorly planned that Narváez would not see the ships again nor the ships him. But he could not bear the thought that people might say he had remained with the ships out of fear. "Under these circumstances," he told Narváez, "I would much rather risk my life than my good name."

A deep rift had opened between the two men. Cabeza de Vaca may have originally admired Narváez and came to mistrust his judgment from events on the journey. Or perhaps Cabeza de Vaca had ambivalent feelings about the governor from the start. For whatever reason, the relationship unraveled at the May 1 meeting. Narváez was, after all, the adelantado—the equivalent of a military commander. He had asked for opinions, and Cabeza de Vaca gave his. To persist in his opposition when the other officers agreed with Narváez's plan was insubordination.

We hear only Cabeza de Vaca's side of this story. His outspokenness sounds courageous, and Narváez's taunt sounds mean and unreasonable. But it is possible that Cabeza de Vaca's stubbornness at the time seemed like arrogance and weakened his chances of getting the wisdom of his advice across to the others.

Had Narváez known that he was on the Florida Peninsula, he might have been wary of an overland expedition. He knew well what Ponce de León and other Spaniards had suffered there. Perhaps lulled into a sense of security because the few indigenous people he had seen were not hostile, he put Cabeza de Vaca's qualms down to inexperience, seeing him as something of a dude, unfamiliar with the "wild west" of conquistador life.

Narváez's decision to march overland while the ships went along the coast was not unreasonable. The conquistador who discovered Río de las Palmas had done just that in 1523. A storm had blown him there when he wanted to reach the Pánuco River farther south. Yet Cabeza de Vaca's advice was worth listening to. Waiting for the ships from Cuba to arrive with supplies and more detailed information about the coast was a good plan.

Narváez's thinking was possibly clouded by visions of gold—a detail he notably omitted from the official report the notary was writing down. He told the notary to say that he had decided to move the camp because the area had too little food to support a settlement. Yet Cabeza de Vaca's account makes it clear that the real goal of marching overland was not finding Río de las Palmas (or another good port) but looking for Apalache. When the expedition left, it headed not south in the direction the brigantine had gone (which Narváez still may not have known was the wrong direction) but in the direction the Indians had pointed—north, toward Apalache.

This 1959 drawing depicts a Spanish explorer traveling through Florida on horseback. While the leaders of the Narváez expedition crossed Florida on horses, most of the party walked.

AN EXPEDITION
TO DISASTER

The overland expedition prepared to leave right away. Three hundred men were each allotted half a pound of salted pork and two pounds of ship's biscuit, or hardtack—a hard, dried bread prepared for long sea voyages. Forty of the men—among them Narváez, the five friars, and the three royal officials—mounted the horses, and the rest traveled on foot.

Meanwhile, one hundred other men and ten women who were wives of men going with Narváez boarded the three ships. One of the women warned Narváez not to go, saying that a Muslim woman in Spain had foretold a disastrous end to the expedition. If he marched inland, she said, neither he nor any of his company would return—or if one should come back, it would be a great miracle. The same woman told the other wives that since their husbands were going to die that they might as well start looking for new mates. She herself planned to do just that. Her pleas and threats did not change

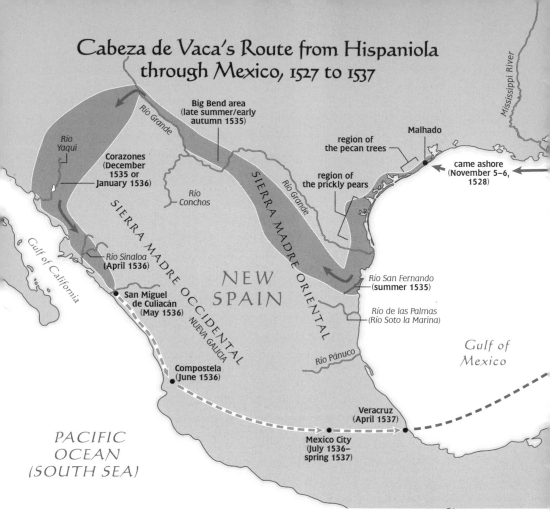

Cabeza de Vaca's Route from Hispaniola through Mexico, 1527 to 1537

Mississippi River

Río Grande

Big Bend area
(late summer/early
autumn 1535)

Malhado

Río
Yaqui

region of
the pecan trees

Corazones
(December
1535 or
January 1536)

Río
Conchos

SIERRA MADRE ORIENTAL

Río Grande

region of
the prickly pears

came ashore
(November 5–6,
1528)

SIERRA MADRE OCCIDENTAL

NUEVA GALICIA

Río Sinaloa
(April 1536)

San Miguel
de Culiacán
(May 1536)

NEW
SPAIN

Gulf of California

Río San Fernando
(summer 1535)

Río de las Palmas
(Río Soto la Marina)

Gulf of
Mexico

Compostela
(June 1536)

Río Pánuco

Veracruz
(April 1537)

PACIFIC
OCEAN
(SOUTH SEA)

Mexico City
(July 1536–
spring 1537)

anything. The men marched inland, and the ships sailed
north along the wild coast. The clueless pilots assured the
passengers that Río de las Palmas was at most fifteen
leagues—about forty-five miles—away.

For the first two weeks, the men lived off the hardtack and
pork, finding only hearts of palm—the tender core of the palmetto plant, sometimes called swamp cabbage—to enliven
their meals. They saw no signs of human life. They were half
starved when they came to a swift river. It took all day to build
rafts for the many men who did not know how to swim. On the
other side, two hundred men armed with bows and arrows

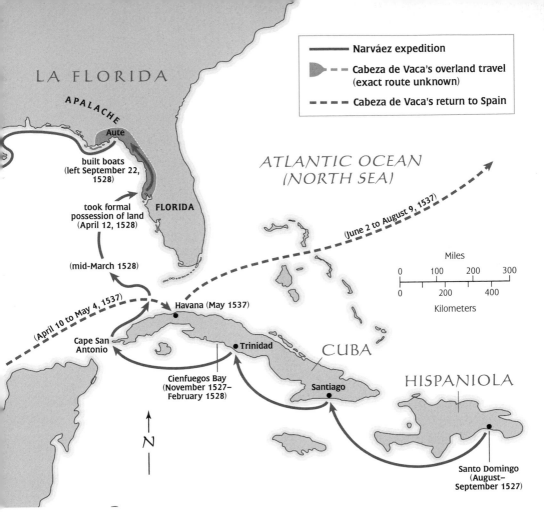

LA FLORIDA

APALACHE

Aute

built boats
(left September 22,
1528)

took formal
possession of land
(April 12, 1528)

FLORIDA

(mid-March 1528)

(April 10 to May 4, 1537)

Cape San
Antonio

Havana (May 1537)

Trinidad

Cienfuegos Bay
(November 1527–
February 1528)

CUBA

Santiago

HISPANIOLA

Santo Domingo
(August–
September 1527)

**ATLANTIC OCEAN
(NORTH SEA)**

(June 2 to August 9, 1537)

Miles

0   100   200   300

0   200   400

Kilometers

N

━━━━━ Narváez expedition

▶ ─ ─ ─ Cabeza de Vaca's overland travel
(exact route unknown)

─ ─ ─ ─ Cabeza de Vaca's return to Spain

suddenly appeared. The Spaniards managed to strike first and captured five or six. The captives took them to their village, where the Spaniards were glad to find large fields of ripe corn.

They remained there several days. During that time, Cabeza de Vaca, the two other royal officials, and Friar Suárez, thinking the river they had crossed might be Río de las Palmas, led a party to the coast to see if there was any harbor. When the search was unsuccessful, the expedition resumed its trek northward, taking the men whom they had captured as guides. For three weeks, the few people they saw fled from them.

On June 17, they met a procession of Indians. Their leader, dressed in painted deerskin, rode on the shoulders of one of his men, and musicians played on reed flutes. The chief offered, through signing, to help them.

Following the Indians, the Spaniards came to another treacherous river, perhaps the Suwannee River, and set to work building a canoe to cross it. One horseman, growing impatient, tried to swim across on his horse. Both man and horse drowned, the first losses since they had set out. While the men mourned their companion, many gratefully ate the horse. Cabeza de Vaca, a true caballero, said he never could bring himself to eat horsemeat.

The friendly chief took them to his village and gave them corn, but that night an arrow narrowly missed one of the Spaniards as he went to get water. Not trusting their hosts, the Spaniards set out again the next day. They soon realized that they were being followed by well-armed warriors. But when the Spaniards tried to ambush them, they vanished into the dense forest.

Lagoons and fallen trees obstructed the Spaniards' way across the flat landscape. Cabeza de Vaca noticed walnut trees, laurels, cedars, live oaks, and palmettos growing in the sandy soil and plentiful wildlife—deer, rabbits, hares, bears, wildcats, opossums (a novelty to the Spaniards), and many types of ducks and birds. But with no leisure to forage for food, the men suffered greatly from hunger.

At last, on June 25, famished and fatigued, they saw a cluster of houses up ahead. Narváez ordered Cabeza de Vaca to attack the village with ten horsemen and fifty foot soldiers. The men found only women and children huddling in about forty grass houses well stocked with dried corn, deer hides, and cloaks of woven cloth. Then, all at once, the Indian men charged into the village firing arrows at them and killing one horse before retreating.

The archers later returned peacefully to ask the Spaniards to give them the women and children. Narváez agreed but seized one of the headmen to hold as a hostage. For four weeks, the Spaniards explored the area while suffering repeated attacks, for the people were angry that Narváez had taken their leader captive. Several Spaniards and horses were wounded, and one expedition member, a native of Texcoco, Mexico, who had come with Friar Suárez, was killed.

This image of a Native American from Florida was created by Jacques Le Moyne, a French artist who accompanied an expedition to the New World in 1565. Almost all of Le Moyne's drawings were burned when the Spanish attacked a French fort in Florida. Le Moyne redrew the pictures from memory upon returning to France.

Cabeza de Vaca was impressed by the Indian archers. "They are wonderfully built, very thin, strong, and agile. Their bows are as thick as an arm, from eleven to twelve spans long, and shoot an arrow at two hundred paces with unerring aim." (A span is the distance from tip of the thumb to the tip of the little finger of an extended hand, about eight to ten inches.) Their arrows flew with such force that they pierced Spanish armor.

Because their guides successfully prevented the Spaniards from discovering larger, more prosperous villages to the west, near the modern city of Tallahassee, they saw only swampy thickets with no sign of gold or any other riches. Disappointed, Narváez decided to leave. The guides told him about Aute, a village on the coast nine days' march to the south, where they would find plenty of food. As the expedition left, Indians followed and harassed them for several days, managing to wound several Spaniards, among them Cabeza de Vaca. Just before they reached Aute, a horseman was killed by an arrow.

Aute was deserted when they arrived but well supplied with corn, squash, and beans. Narváez sent Cabeza de Vaca to look for the sea with two captains, Alonso del Castillo and Andrés Dorantes, Friar Suárez, and seven other horsemen and fifty foot soldiers. They found an inlet where they stopped to feast on oysters, but further exploration suggested that the coast was still far off. While they were gone, Indians attacked Aute, and Narváez, along with many others, fell ill.

The situation was turning desperate. Deciding that Aute was unsafe, the whole camp moved together with great difficulty to the inlet where Cabeza de Vaca had found the oysters. Narváez asked each member of the expedition what to do next. Remaining where they were was no solution. Fully one-third of the men were gravely ill, and more were falling sick every hour. With the possibility of a mass death staring them in the face, they decided to build boats and leave.

"This seemed impossible to everyone," Cabeza de Vaca noted, "since none of us knew how to build them. We had no tools, no iron, no [forge], no oakum [tarred plant fibers used for packing seams], no pitch, no [ropes for rigging], in sum, nothing of what was indispensable. Neither was there anyone to instruct us in shipbuilding, and above all, there was nothing for those who would have to perform these tasks to eat while the work was going on."

God provided (Cabeza de Vaca wrote later) that the next day one man offered to make a bellows from tubes of wood and deerskin. With a bellows, they could make a fire hot enough to melt down stirrups, spurs, crossbows, and other iron objects. From this iron, they could make nails, saws, axes, and other tools. Others also came forward to offer their talents. A Portuguese carpenter in the company designed and directed work on the boats. An expedition member from Greece, Doroteo Teodoro, knew how to extract pitch from pine trees to waterproof the vessels. Other workers felled and planed trees for lumber, gathered palmetto fronds to shred into oakum to fill gaps between the planks, wove the hair from horses' tails and manes into ropes for rigging the sails, and fashioned sails from shirts.

Horsemen who were not sick raided Aute for food, making off with 640 bushels of dried corn. Other men gathered shellfish from the inlet. Every third day, a horse was slaughtered to feed the workers and the sick. The skin was stripped off horses' legs in one piece and tanned to make bags for storing freshwater.

A modern artist has pictured how shipwrecked men sewed shirts together to make sails, melted iron objects to make nails, and built wooden boats in the hopes of continuing their journey on sea.

Twice Indians attacked men gathering shellfish, killing ten with their powerful arrows. Another forty men died from sickness and starvation.

On September 20, almost seven weeks after they began building them, five boats, each about thirty-three feet long, were ready to go. Between forty-seven and forty-nine men were assigned to each boat. Cabeza de Vaca and the inspector Diego de Solís shared command of the fifth boat. Two days later, after killing the last horse for meat on the journey, they embarked. Loaded with the men, weapons, armor, and provisions, the boats sank so deep that only seven or eight inches showed above the waterline. "We were so crowded," Cabeza de Vaca wrote, "we could not even move."

For a week, they rowed through coves and inlets (probably near Apalachee Bay on the coast of the Florida Panhandle). At last, on September 29, they reached open water. On an island at the mouth of the bay, they found an empty settlement with plenty of fish and dried fish eggs to eat and five abandoned canoes. Using wood from the canoes, they raised the sides of their boats, adding ten more inches of protection against waves. They then sailed out into the Gulf of Mexico and set their course westward. At that point, they seem to have known that it was the right direction to go to reach Río de las Palmas, but they probably still had no idea how far away it was.

Weeks passed as they made their way along the coast, sometimes going for days without freshwater. The horse-leg water bags rotted, and when they went ashore, they could not always find springs or streams. At one point, they were trapped by a great storm on an island with nothing to drink, and five men died from drinking salt water.

At last they came to a settlement where unarmed people greeted them with pottery jars of water and cooked fish—"It was our Lord's pleasure, who many a time shows his favor in the hour of greatest misfortune," Cabeza de Vaca said. Narváez offered them dried corn and "some trinkets" in return. As destitute as the Spaniards were, they still had beads, little bells, and colorful caps to give Indians, trifles that were as much a part of their survival gear as corn, boots, and armor. Sick Spaniards rested on the beach as Narváez, and several officers entered the chief's lodge for a friendly meal.

When night fell, their hosts attacked. Narváez and the officers tried to seize the chief as a hostage, but he escaped, leaving the Spaniards holding his fine fur cape. The Spaniards rushed to their boats, helping Narváez, who had been struck in the face with a stone. Cabeza de Vaca

In this engraving (based on a watercolor by Le Moyne), de Bry shows Floridian Indians in dugout canoes bringing their harvest to a storehouse built of stones and earth and roofed with mud-plastered palm fronds.

remained on the beach with fifty men to fend off three more assaults during the night. Every Spaniard was wounded. During the last onset, three captains took fifteen men to set up an ambush and surprised their attackers from the rear. The people then fled inland. Cabeza de Vaca broke up their canoes to build fires to protect them from cold north winds. These winds prevented the Spaniards from sailing away until the next morning.

Three days later, their water once again used up, the Spaniards entered an the mouth of a river. Seeing a canoe, they asked the people in it for water. The people agreed to fill their containers. Cabeza de Vaca does not explain what they were using to hold water. Perhaps they had some of the pottery jars from their earlier stop.

The Greek, Doroteo Teodoro, insisted on going with the

Indians to get the water, although the others urged him not to, and an African man went with him. Two Indians remained in one of the boats as hostages. When the Indians later returned with empty containers and neither Teodoro nor the African, the two hostages tried to leap into the water, but the Spaniards held them back.

The next day, many Indians paddled out in canoes to demand the return of their two men. Narváez agreed on condition that they return Teodoro and the African. The Indians, several of whom wore fur capes that seemed to indicate high rank, urged the Spaniards to come ashore, where they offered to return the two men as well as give everyone water and other things.

Meanwhile, more canoes were gathering in the bay. Afraid that the Indians would block them from returning to the open sea, the Spaniards set sail, leaving the two men behind. All were "very despondent and saddened by the loss of those two Christians."

Some days later, the boats came to a very large river, the Mississippi, which poured in a torrent into the sea. Wind and current prevented them from landing to build fires and toast their raw corn. After battling these forces for three days, Cabeza de Vaca awoke one morning to find his boat separated from the others. Their stone anchors had not been heavy enough to hold the boats in place. That afternoon he spied two other boats. In the closer one was Narváez, who asked Cabeza de Vaca what he thought they should do.

As earlier, Cabeza de Vaca believed that keeping the group together was essential for their survival. He proposed that the two boats should join the third one. Narváez disagreed. He wanted to head for land to get water and food, and the third boat was farther out to sea. Narváez ordered

Cabeza de Vaca to start rowing and follow him.

But Narváez had stronger and healthier men in his boat (as well as a lighter load, according to Oviedo), and Cabeza de Vaca and his men could not keep up. Seeing that, Cabeza de Vaca asked Narváez if they could tie the boats together. Narváez refused.

Cabeza de Vaca asked what Narváez was commanding him to do. Narváez replied "that this was no time for orders; that each one should do the best he could to save himself, which is what he intended to do." And with that parting shot, Narváez ordered his men to row toward shore.

As Narváez rowed out of sight, Cabeza de Vaca sailed toward the other boat. Its captains, Peñalosa and Téllez, agreed to join him, and the two boats sailed together for four days on a daily ration of half a handful of raw corn for each man. Then a storm separated them.

Left alone in the cold wind, hungry and ill, the men in Cabeza de Vaca's boat lay in a heap, many unconscious. Cabeza de Vaca and a man he refers to as the skipper took turns at the helm through the night. Near dawn, they heard breakers and decided to land when it turned light. Cabeza de Vaca wrote:

> Close to shore a wave took us and hurled the boat a horseshoe's throw out of the water. With the violent shock nearly all the people who lay in the boat like dead came to themselves, and, seeing we were close to land, began to crawl out on all fours. When they got out they climbed into a rocky area, where we built a fire and toasted some of our corn. We found rainwater, and with the warmth of the fire people revived and began to cheer up. The day we arrived there was the sixth of the month of November.

STRANDED
IN TEXAS

After their meager meal, Cabeza de Vaca sent his strongest man to climb a tall tree to see what he could learn about their location. He returned with the news that they were on an island. Historians calculate the island was somewhere in or near Galveston Bay, off the southeastern coast of Texas. The ground looked trampled, the man reported, certain that they had reached Spanish territory.

Cabeza de Vaca ordered him to search more carefully. Finding Indian huts, he stole some fish, a small dog, and a cooking pot. Three men saw him and followed him back to the beach, where they sat observing the strangers. Soon others joined them. Before long Cabeza de Vaca and his starving boat mates were facing a hundred archers, tall, brown-skinned, bare-chested men with long reeds, "as thick as two fingers" pierced through their nipples and shorter, thinner ones jutting from their lower lips.

The Spaniards had no way to defend themselves. Barely six of them could stand up. Cabeza de Vaca and Diego de Solís approached the strangers cautiously, holding out beads and bells as a friendly offering. In return, each man gave them one arrow, which Cabeza de Vaca welcomed as a sign of peaceful intent. Using gestures, the Indians told them that they would return the next day with food.

The next morning at sunrise, the Indians arrived with plenty of fish and some edible roots that tasted like walnuts. In the evening, they returned again with food and water. This time women, dressed in Spanish moss, came too, with children who gaped at the strange visitors. For several days, the Native Americans cared for the shipwrecked Europeans camped on the beach.

Recovering their strength, the Spaniards decided to continue their journey toward Mexico, hoping either to find the ships at Río de las Palmas or to reach the Spanish province of Pánuco farther down the coast. They dug their boat out of the sand and reloaded their few supplies. But when they tried to relaunch the boat, they lost everything to a rogue wave. Diego de Solís and two others drowned when the boat overturned.

That evening, not knowing that the Spaniards planned to leave, the islanders again brought them food and were shocked to find them naked on the beach with the bodies of their drowned comrades. They immediately sat down and wept loudly. Their compassion for the castaways amazed Cabeza de Vaca. For all his experience with Canarians in Spain and with Native Americans in Cuba, Florida, and along the Gulf Coast, he still saw them as something other than wholly human. To him the Indians were "beings . . . devoid of reason, uneducated, . . . [and] brutish"; yet their tears showed him that they were capable of being "deeply moved by pity for us."

Cabeza de Vaca probably misinterpreted their motive for weeping. Most likely, the Indians had noticed the dead men and were carrying out a mourning ritual. Although we know nothing more about the people who lived on the Texas coast in the early sixteenth century than what Cabeza de Vaca wrote about them, later explorers also came across groups of Native Americans for whom weeping was an important ritual.

The Spaniards had lost everything. Worse, they were in immediate danger of dying from malnutrition and exposure. As their leader, Cabeza de Vaca knew that the sole choice was to ask the Indians to take them in. Some expedition members had been in Mexico with Cortés and feared that these Indians, like the Aztecs, would sacrifice captives to stone idols. Cabeza de Vaca decided to take that risk, for "death was surer and nearer" if they remained on the beach.

By then adept at sign language, Cabeza de Vaca asked the local inhabitants to take them to their lodges. They seemed eager to do this but gestured for the Spaniards to wait. After gathering firewood, about thirty of them left the beach. The rest remained with the Spaniards. Late in the day, they all set out together at a rapid pace, and the puzzled Spaniards discovered the reason for the delay:

> To ward off the cold, they had provided four or five big fires on the road and at each one they warmed us, lest on the way some one of us might faint or die. As soon as they saw we had regained a little warmth and strength they would carry us to the next fire with such haste that our feet barely touched the ground.

That night the Indians celebrated with dancing. Although warmed by many fires, the Spaniards shivered with apprehension. For all they knew, the feasting and dancing were the opening act of a bloody ritual in which they would be sacrificial victims. The Indians, however, were probably performing some kind of initiation or adoption rite to make the rescued Europeans members of their group. By taking the foreigners into their community, they would add workers and warriors and gain whatever skills and possible magic powers the strangers possessed. After a sleepless night worrying they might be killed, the Spaniards were much relieved the next morning when their hosts served them fish and roots just as they had on earlier days.

The first day in the village, Cabeza de Vaca noticed a man wearing a trinket unlike ones he had distributed. Asking where he obtained it, Cabeza de Vaca learned that there were other Europeans in the area. He sent two of his men with two guides to meet them. The Europeans turned out to be Captains Andrés Dorantes and Alonso del Castillo and all their boat mates. They had been stranded about five miles to the east. Their boat was wrecked, but they had not lost anything.

After a joyful reunion, Cabeza de Vaca, Dorantes, and Castillo decided to repair the boat and send the strongest men in it to get help from Nuño de Guzmán, the Spanish governor of the province of Pánuco. The rest would walk along the coast as soon as they had recovered enough for the journey.

The Spaniards eagerly set to work, but when they launched the boat, it sank, taking with it any hope of a sea journey. As difficult as it had been, traveling by boat was easier and safer than hiking on land.

The weather remained cold, and since so many men lacked clothing and gear for an overland trek, it seemed best to remain where they were for the winter. The four healthiest men agreed to walk to Pánuco to take news of their misfortunes. All knew how to swim, an important skill for getting across the many waterways along the coast.

No sooner had the four men set out with a local guide than a bitter cold spell began. Ice storms froze the shallow ponds where the Indians harvested the nut-flavored roots and speared the fish that were their staple foods. Cabeza de Vaca does not say how large the population was, only that there were two different groups, the Han and the Cavoques, but it was too small to easily absorb about eighty or ninety newcomers during the least abundant season of the year. Their rescuers housed the castaways in various dwellings scattered around the island and expected the healthier ones to help look for food and water.

The Spaniards—especially those who had lost clothes in the failed attempt to sail away—found flimsy huts of woven grasses inadequate shelter against the cold. Malnourished and hungry, men began to die. Five of the Spaniards, quartered together near the coast, ate one another as each one died, until there was only one left alive. Their cannibalism shocked their hosts.

The Indians began to fall ill too, suffering stomach ailments from which half of them died. Typhus germs from Europe might have caused the epidemic. Suspecting the Spaniards of causing their illness, some plotted to kill the newcomers. Cabeza de Vaca's host, however, pointed out that Spaniards were dying as well and argued it was hardly worth killing the few who remained alive.

The Indians then insisted that Cabeza de Vaca and other

survivors help cure the sick. Cabeza de Vaca joked that they expected the Spaniards to be physicians "without any examination or asking for our diplomas." But the Indians were serious. They withheld food from the Spaniards until they agreed to do what they could. Giving in from hunger, the Spaniards made signs of the cross over the sick, recited the Lord's Prayer and the Hail Mary, and prayed for God "to give them good health and inspire them to treat us well." By this means, they produced enough cures to receive rewards of animal skins, which provided some relief from the winter weather.

Prayers, however, did not save the Christians. Within a short time after their arrival, only fifteen of the ninety or so Europeans remained. As their number dwindled, the survivors took to calling the island Malhado—"Bad Luck" Island.

ESCAPE FROM MALHADO

The Han and the Cavoques did not live on the island all year. Every two or three months, they rolled up their grass mat homes and moved to another area. The nut-flavored roots on Malhado were best to harvest in November and December, before they sprouted new shoots. In February the two groups paddled dugout canoes to the mainland, where for three months they lived off oysters found along the bays. A monthlong celebration feasting on blackberries followed. Cabeza de Vaca does not say how they spent the other five months of the year. No doubt they moved periodically to new sources of fish, nuts, or fruits in a seasonal pattern that was repeated every year.

The Han and the Cavoques spoke different languages and foraged at different sites, so that the Spaniards went separate ways depending on which group they traveled with. Cabeza de Vaca lost contact with Dorantes, Castillo, and the other survivors during the oyster season, and while Cabeza de Vaca was on the mainland, he became terribly ill.

In April 1529, the fourteen other survivors returned to Malhado. Dorantes and Castillo gathered them all together from their scattered lodges to start out for Pánuco. Two of them were too ill to travel, so the others set forth without them. They paid an Indian the fur cape that they had taken from the chief on their coastal journey the year before to ferry them across the channel to the mainland and take them to where Cabeza de Vaca was being cared for.

Only much later, when Cabeza de Vaca finally recovered from his illness, did he learn from his hosts that the twelve expedition members had come and then departed. He had been too sick to see them. Now it was too late to try to catch up with them. It seemed wiser to regain his strength and travel later with the other two when they all got well.

As Cabeza de Vaca's health improved, however, his hosts forced him to work harder, giving him the most difficult jobs and treating him like a slave. No longer able to stand having his bare skin shredded as he trudged through sharp reeds to dig up roots growing underwater, he decided to escape to the Charrucan Indians, who lived in forests on the mainland.

The Charrucans apparently traded with the Han and the Cavoques, for Cabeza de Vaca knew about their needs. Aware that the Charrucans prized shell beads and shell knives, which they used to harvest "a beanlike fruit" (perhaps mesquite), he took seashells to exchange for deer hides, red ochre dye, flint (to make arrow points), glue and hard canes (to make arrows), and decorative tassels made from deer hair. Cabeza de Vaca knew people living along the coast desired these inland products, which he traded for more shells and fish from the sea.

The Charrucans harvested a "beanlike fruit," likely mesquite (left), with shell knives made from the seashells traded to them by Cabeza de Vaca.

By becoming a trader, Cabeza de Vaca enjoyed the freedom to go where he liked and won the respect of all the Native American groups in the region. He also became well acquainted with the countryside and how to survive in it. He learned Indian languages and heard about other Indian groups living farther south. The experience was good training for his upcoming journey to Pánuco.

On a return visit to Malhado, however, Cabeza de Vaca discovered that one of the Spaniards left behind had died and the other was reluctant to leave because he was unable to swim. Each year Cabeza de Vaca came back to try to convince the Spaniard to leave. At last, in the spring of 1533—

four and a half years after the waves had tossed them onto Malhado Island—the man agreed to join Cabeza de Vaca on a trek to Pánuco.

The trip began well. Cabeza de Vaca was familiar with the territory. In his years as a trader, he had become friendly with the Deaguanes people, who lived south of Malhado. The Deaguanes accompanied the two Spaniards to the southern edge of their territory, an inlet Cabeza de Vaca called Espíritu Santo (Holy Ghost). This was perhaps Cavallo Pass, which connects Texas's Matagorda Bay with the Gulf of Mexico.

On the shore across the inlet, they met a group called the Quevenes. From them they learned that all the Spaniards who had left Malhado in 1528 and 1529 had died of cold or hunger or been killed by Indians, except three—Dorantes, Castillo, and Castillo's African slave Estevanico. They were still alive, the Quevenes said, but "in very sorry condition," for they were constantly kicked and beaten by the people they lived with. The Quevenes offered to show them where the Indians who held these men would be gathering pecans. The Quevenes also demonstrated how badly the three men were being treated by kicking and beating the two Spaniards.

It was too much for the other Spaniard. Afraid the Quevenes would kill them, he chose to return to Malhado. Several Deaguanes women traveling with them agreed to take him back. Nothing Cabeza de Vaca could say would change his mind. He departed with the women, and Cabeza de Vaca went on alone with the Quevenes.

In two days, Cabeza de Vaca and the Quevenes reached groves of tall pecan trees with widespread branches near (it is thought) the Guadalupe River. Here an Indian—Cabeza de Vaca did not know what group he belonged to—helped him find Andrés Dorantes, who was living with the Mariames. He was astounded to see Cabeza de Vaca alive. "We gave many thanks to God for being together again and that day was one of the happiest we enjoyed in all our days."

The Indian also brought Cabeza de Vaca to Castillo and Estevanico, who were living with the Yguaces, another native group that came to the "River of Nuts" to feast on pecans. As the four men rejoiced to have found one another, Dorantes told Cabeza de Vaca news of other members of the Narváez expedition. When Dorantes and the eleven others were traveling south four years earlier, in the spring of 1529, they came upon Figueroa, one of the four who left Malhado with a local guide late in 1528. His companions and the guide had all died of the severe cold and hunger, except one Spaniard, who was killed by Indians when he tried to run away from them.

Figueroa had met another Spaniard, Hernando de Esquivel, who told him the fates of two of the other boats. These boats had also been tossed ashore by the November storm, only farther down the coast. One was wrecked, but the other, Narváez's boat, remained seaworthy. The ninety or so men set up camp together, but Narváez and two others chose to sleep aboard the boat. That night a fierce north wind blew the boat out to sea. It was the last anyone saw of the boat and its three passengers.

That winter the rest died of cold and hunger. Only Esquivel survived by eating those who died. Then the Mariames captured him.

When Figueroa met Esquivel later that spring, he urged him to escape his captors and go with him to Pánuco. But the two men disagreed on which direction to go. So Esquivel stayed with the Mariames and Figueroa traveled south along the coast, where he met Dorantes and the others with him.

Figueroa and a priest traveling with Dorantes later set off

together for Pánuco. Indians captured the rest of Dorantes's small band and distributed them among several groups. Over the next four years, Dorantes had heard rumors that some had starved and others had been slain, among them Esquivel. Dorantes's own captors, the Mariames, had shown him Esquivel's sword, rosary, prayer book, and other things of his that they had kept after killing him.

Hearing all these stories must have been distressing for Cabeza de Vaca. In his report, however, Cabeza de Vaca refrained from criticizing Narváez for the many mistakes that had brought the expedition so much loss. Oviedo judged Narváez more harshly when he recorded the same events. "It seems to me," Oviedo wrote, "he knew not how to govern himself. Can there be greater folly than to listen to and follow such leaders? . . . Oh cursed gold! Oh treasures and gains so dangerous! Oh fine sables! . . . bought with blood and their lives and they were not even brought back."

Yet Narváez, the incompetent leader of the whole fiasco, had perhaps reached a safe port in his boat. And there was one boat still unaccounted for: the boat commanded by Captains Peñalosa and Téllez. Perhaps even Figueroa and the priest were still alive somewhere. But it must have seemed unlikely to Cabeza de Vaca that any of the expedition members had reached Pánuco. No Spanish ships had come to rescue them.

As they gathered and cracked pecans to grind with a few wild grains for food, the four survivors considered their own chances of ever reaching home. Dorantes had a plan. During the late summer, he explained to Cabeza de Vaca, many native groups met in a region where prickly pears grew in abundance. For several months, they fed on this juicy, seed-filled fruit of the nopal cactus. Here the Spaniards would have the

The red fruits of this nopal cactus, called prickly pears, are juicy and sweet, although full of seeds. Nopal cacti grow in Texas, the southwestern United States, and Mexico. Native Americans of this region would gather when the fruits were ripe and plentiful. Cabeza de Vaca and the other Spaniards hoped to meet up with other Indian groups at this annual gathering.

chance to meet with Indians from farther south and arrange to leave with them when the prickly pear season was over.

A good plan, Cabeza de Vaca thought. He knew that they had to depend on Native American allies to make their way. So he submitted to remaining with the Mariames, who held Dorantes, even though it meant once again becoming a slave. When the pecan season drew to an end, the men went their separate ways, Cabeza de Vaca and Dorantes with the Mariames and Castillo and Estevanico with the Yguaces.

Cabeza de Vaca hated living with the Mariames, whom he described as cruel masters, thieves, liars, and drunkards. They killed all girl children and bought wives from enemies, paying either a good bow and two arrows or a large fishing net for each wife. These purchased women did all the work of gathering and preparing food, fetching water, and carrying firewood and other loads. Food was scarce. Often they went three or four days without eating. Bitter roots, the staple of their diet, were difficult to digest even after long roasting.

"Their hunger is so great," Cabeza de Vaca wrote, "that they eat spiders and ant eggs, worms, lizards and salamanders and serpents, and vipers whose bite is fatal. They eat earth and wood, and anything they can get, including deer dung and other things I do not wish to mention. I truly believe from what I saw that if there were any stones in the country they would eat them as well."

That summer of 1533, the plan to escape failed. Before the four had a chance to contact Indians from the south, a quarrel broke out between the Mariames and the Yguaces over a woman and the two groups packed up their mat houses and left. Cabeza de Vaca and the others faced another year in wretched captivity. Cabeza de Vaca found the ordeal so unbearable that he ran off three times. But each time, his captors pursued and captured him.

The following year, in mid-September, the four men reunited with the help of Indian allies. These men showed them Spanish clothing and weapons that they had bartered for with the Camones, a group that lived along the coast. The Camones, they said, had come upon the emaciated crew of a shipwrecked boat six years earlier and had killed them all. Peñalosa and Téllez had apparently made it as far as Padre Island off the coast of Corpus Christi, Texas. The men in the boat that had gone the farthest—they were still about four hundred miles from Pánuco, however—had received the worst treatment of all. It was a timely warning to the four survivors. The Camones were a group to avoid.

AMONG THE AVAVARES

For two days, the four men enjoyed the last of the prickly pears in the hot September weather, made hotter by the smoky fires built to ward off mosquitoes. "During the entire time we ate prickly pears we were thirsty," Cabeza de Vaca remembered later. "To allay our thirst we drank the fruit's juice, first pouring it into a pit, which we dug in the soil, and when that was full drinking to satisfaction."

As the season drew to a close, they struck out on their own and walked south through fields of nopal cactus. Spying smoke on the horizon, they headed toward it hoping to find the Avavares, who brought bows to trade with the Mariames and who would soon be traveling farther south. More important, the Avavares camped inland, away from the hostile groups that lived on the coast.

The Avavares spoke a different language but understood

what the Spaniards said in the Mariames tongue. They welcomed the four travelers with gifts of prickly pears and gave them lodging.

That night some Avavares begged Castillo to cure them of headaches. Castillo made the sign of the cross over them and commended them to God. Immediately, they said all their pain was gone. They gratefully brought him prickly pears and a piece of venison—something Cabeza de Vaca had not seen in so long that at first he did not know what it was. The news spread, and others came to be healed, bringing more meat than the four survivors knew what to do with. Then the whole group danced and celebrated all night and for the next three days.

The Spaniards asked their hosts about the land to the south. When told that they would find nothing to eat on their

This engraving by de Bry is based on a painting by Le Moyne. Many Native American groups, such as the Avavares of south-central Texas, depended on deer for food and hides.

own, they opted to stay with the Avavares until spring. Since the Avavares hunted deer, it would give the Spaniards a chance to acquire hides for clothing and bedding for their journey.

Several days later, the Avavares moved to another area to harvest mesquite beans. While looking for the long, leathery pods, Cabeza de Vaca became separated from the group. Unable to find his way back to the camp as dusk fell, Cabeza de Vaca wrote, "It pleased God to let me find a burning tree." He kept warm by its fire through the chilly night. The next day, he gathered a load of firewood and set out with two burning torches to find his friends. He searched for them for days. Each night he dug a hole and built four fires around it and then bundled dried grasses to cover himself with and lay down in the hole to sleep. One night a spark set the dry grass, on fire and Cabeza de Vaca leaped up to save himself from burning to death. For the rest of his life, he bore scars on his scalp from the accident. At last, after five days, he found his friends, who had given him up for dead.

This harrowing experience left Cabeza de Vaca scarred yet strengthened. His faith in God grew deeper. "God had mercy upon me," he wrote of the ordeal, "that in all this time there was no norther [a fast-moving cold front from the north] or I could not have survived." He began to feel strongly that his survival had some special purpose. Narváez's conquest may have failed, but Cabeza de Vaca and his three companions still had a role to play in what they viewed as God's plans for the New World.

As they traveled with the Avavares and met other native groups, news of Castillo's cures spread. One day some warlike Indians asked Castillo to go with them to heal a wounded man. Perhaps afraid of what might happen should his cure fail, Castillo hesitated to go, so they asked Cabeza de Vaca instead. He arrived to find the man's relatives mourning his death. The man's eyes were rolled back and he had no pulse, but Cabeza de Vaca nevertheless said prayers for him. The Indians paid him with a bow and baskets of prickly pears. After returning to the Avavares camp, Cabeza de Vaca learned that the man had recovered.

This remarkable incident brought still more people asking to be cured or blessed, and Dorantes and Estevanico joined in to handle the crowds. "We never treated anyone that did not afterward say he was well," Cabeza de Vaca reported later, "and they had such confidence in our skill that they believed that none of them would die as long as we were among them."

Cabeza de Vaca seemed to understand the role that expectation plays in healing. We do not know exactly what it was about the four survivors of the Narváez expedition that made so many Native Americans see them as great healers with mystical powers. They did not have horses or guns to strike awe into the Indians. By the time the survivors reached the Avavares, the paler skin of the Spaniards was no doubt well browned by the sun, and if they wore anything at all— both Cabeza de Vaca and Oviedo frequently speak of their being naked and barefoot—it would have been what the people around them wore.

Yet they did look unusual. The Spaniards had hairy faces and may have had blue eyes and red or blond hair. Estevanico's skin was black. Cabeza de Vaca frequently describes Indians he met as tall, which suggests that the Europeans were smaller than they were.

More important, when the Avavares bartered with coastal Indians, they heard of the Spaniards' marvelous cures. They perhaps also listened to descriptions of objects found on Spanish victims, strange objects such as Esquivel's sword, rosary, and prayer book. The sharp blade of a sword, the strange beads to which the Christians uttered incantations, and the papers they read from or made marks on all had magic potential easily exaggerated by rumor.

Whatever created their belief, the Avavares embraced it wholeheartedly. People who received the cures felt better because they expected to and because the whole community supported this result with their expectations as well. Cabeza de Vaca realized that this faith would help them reach Pánuco. It would also help them to carry out their mission as conquistadors. Had they not come to the New World to bring Christianity to people who lived in darkness?

While Cabeza de Vaca was with the Avavares, they told him a strange story about a fearsome creature that appeared many years before and mutilated people. The creature was short and bearded, and his sudden appearance made the Indians' hair stand on end. After cutting open their abdomens with a large flint knife, he sliced off part of their intestines and tossed it into the fire. Then the creature placed his hands on the wound, and it closed at once. Several Indians showed Cabeza de Vaca scars as proof of the existence of this "Evil Thing," as they called it. The Spaniards laughed at first. But realizing how intense the belief in this creature was and how afraid the people were of its return, they explained it as the devil. They also promised that Christianity would destroy the power of this creature.

The eight months Cabeza de Vaca and his companions spent with the Avavares were grueling. They suffered greatly from hunger, for the Avavares had "neither corn nor acorns or walnuts," and with no access to the coast, they had no fish either. Two or three times a year, the Indians would hunt for deer and enjoy feasts of venison. Most of the time, they subsisted on roots. "The children around there," Oviedo reported, "are so thin and bloated that they look like toads."

Noticing how foraging for food took up so much of the Avavares's time that they had no time for other work, Cabeza de Vaca arranged to make combs, arrows, bows, nets, and reed matting for their huts in exchange for food. One task he particularly appreciated was scraping and tanning, because then he "scraped it very deeply in order to eat the parings, which would last me two or three days."

When the Avavares paid the Spaniards for their work with meat, they learned to eat it raw at once. Otherwise, if they put it on a fire to broil, "the first Indian who came along would snatch it away and eat it."

As difficult as life was, at least the Avavares did not enslave their guests. "Among these Indians," Oviedo wrote, "they were well treated and were free to do as they pleased." At last the prickly pears began to ripen. It was the summer of 1535. Eager to be on their way, the four survivors "fled with care and secrecy." For the first time since the shipwreck on Malhado in 1528 and the failed attempt to travel overland to Pánuco in 1529, the four felt well enough supplied to undertake a steady journey toward Spanish settlements. They knew it was important to seize their chance and not risk further delay.

CROSSING
THE COUNTRY

In August 1535, Cabeza de Vaca and the three other survivors slipped away from the Avavares and began to travel from one Indian settlement to the next. They spent a few days here and there along the way whenever their hosts had food to give them—usually the thick, round leaves of the nopal cactus, prickly pears (roasted because they were not yet ripe), or mesquite beans pounded into a flour and mixed with earth and water. Cabeza de Vaca does not say what the various Indians called themselves. Perhaps since he was spending less time with these groups, he did not recall their names clearly when he wrote his account later.

Everywhere they went, the inhabitants brought their sick to be cured and wept when the Spaniards bid them good-bye. Word of their travels preceded them, and Indian groups they had not yet visited sent women to guide them to their settlements. Women came because the groups were all at war with one another. As noncombatants, women could carry messages or goods between hostile groups.

Their men went about armed and watchful. When they camped near enemies, they set their huts at the edge of thickets and dug trenches close by where they slept, hidden by piles of brushwood, ready to retaliate if enemies attacked their empty huts. Their military preparedness reminded Cabeza de Vaca of his days fighting for King Ferdinand. These people "are so astute in guarding themselves from an enemy," he wrote, "that it seems as if they had trained in Italy and in continuous warfare."

One afternoon the four travelers crossed a big river, as wide as the Guadalquivir in Seville, with a swift current and water deep enough to reach their chests as they waded across. They were probably crossing the Rio Grande—today the border between Mexico and the United States—just inland from the Gulf Coast.

The first village they reached had one hundred or more huts. The people mobbed the newcomers, almost crushing them to death in their excitement to see them. The villagers danced and celebrated all night, making music with gourds filled with small pebbles. They valued the gourds highly because they mysteriously appeared floating in the river during spring floods. The people believed the gourds came from the sky, which Cabeza de Vaca discovered was often the explanation given for the origin of unfamiliar things and people.

The next day, "every living soul of the village" not only came to be touched and blessed with the sign of the cross by the Spaniards but also followed after them when they left to walk farther south. The followers then took payment from people in the next village who hoped to be cured.

The number of followers swelled as the four men traveled. People accompanying them began to ransack the homes of people who received the travelers. Cabeza de Vaca felt sorry for those being robbed and feared the pilfering would cause trouble, but their hosts assured him that it was no problem. They would repay themselves at the next village by walking with them and taking what belonged to those who lived there.

Proceeding in this fashion, the travelers began to see mountains on the horizon, the first mountains they had come upon since landing on the North American continent seven years earlier. At this point, they estimated that they were about forty-five miles inland from the Gulf. When they reached a river, some of their followers urged them to go downstream to where they had relatives, but the four men refused, electing instead to go upriver so as not to risk encountering the hostile Indians they had heard lived along the coast. The travelers were still headed south, but it was the first of a series of choices that soon deflected their course.

"We preferred to cross the countryside, since further inland, [the people] were in better condition and treated us better," Cabeza de Vaca wrote later. "We also felt sure that we would find the country more thickly settled and with more resources. In the end, we did this because, in crossing the country, we would see much more of its particulars, so that, in case God our Lord should be pleased to spare one of us and take him back to a land of Christians, he might give an account of it."

The decision the travelers made to "cross the country" meant that instead of heading directly to Pánuco, roughly two hundred miles south of where they were at that time, they were going to walk almost fifteen hundred miles to the west coast of Mexico. Instead of walking on a coastal plain, they would traverse two major mountain ranges, the Sierra Madre Oriental and the Sierra Madre Occidental, as well as the high desert plateau between.

It was not, apparently, a clear-cut decision made at one point in the trail. At first, they wanted to avoid unfriendly Indians along the coast. As they followed the river upstream into foothills, it led them to the southwest. They gradually shifted course when the river veered west and then northwest. Perhaps they hoped a branch of the river would lead them south. Or perhaps simple curiosity drew them further westward.

Soon their new course gained a sense of purpose. One of the goals of the Narváez expedition, after all, had been to locate the west coast of North America. The four survivors of the expedition had no way of knowing how far it would be, but that did not matter. After the ordeals of illness, enslavement, and hunger on the coast of Texas, they were free. They also had the support of large numbers of Native Americans. The king had granted Narváez a license to explore this very area. Now his treasurer, two captains, and one slave were ready to carry out what Narváez had failed to do with the six hundred men he had recruited in Spain eight years earlier. They were no longer refugees struggling to reach Spanish civilization. They were once again conquistadors. These were most unusual conquistadors—barefoot, unarmed, and peaceful—but still loyal servants of their king, church, and country.

As they traveled across what are now the Mexican states of Tamaulipas and Nuevo León, their guides told the people living along the way that the four strangers were children of the sun and had the power to cure the sick or to kill them all. Give the four strangers all your possessions, they said, and show them other places where people live. Since the travelers took only what they needed for food and gave everything else to their guides, each group profited.

In one settlement, two healers gave the Spaniards gourds. These they kept because, as Cabeza de Vaca explained, the gourds "greatly added to our authority since they hold these ceremonial objects in high regard."

In this fashion, the conquistadors and their constantly changing guides followed the slopes of the mountains in a northwesterly direction. The people they met, like those who lived on the Texas coast, were hunters and gatherers who foraged over specific areas, carrying their mat houses with them. The people here, however, were apparently better fed and supplied, at least during the summer months.

After traveling inland for more than 150 miles, as estimated by Cabeza de Vaca (Oviedo's version says 240 miles, which is likely closer to the truth), the four men came to a settlement—probably in east central Coahuila—where an Indian gave Andrés Dorantes a copper rattle with a face on it.

Amazed to see evidence of copper mining and metal casting, the Spaniards asked where it came from. The Indians gestured to the northwest, indicating as well that copper abounded there. Although it lacked the allure of gold, copper ranked high on the Spanish list of desirable metals, for it was useful in processing silver, building ships, making guns, and minting coins. The same Indians also gave them blankets of woven cotton, the first Native American cloth the Spaniards had seen since leaving the Florida Peninsula.

As they moved on, traveling "among so many different tribes and languages that nobody's memory can recall them all," many Indians did not return to their accustomed lands but joined the Spaniards and Estevanico. Soon each conquistador had a retinue of men and women who looked after his needs. The men clubbed hares or shot deer with arrows and built ovens to broil the meat. The women wove mats for their lodging. At times the followers numbered three or four thousand people, none of whom would eat until the four travelers had blessed their food.

Crossing another great river—either the Babia or the Sabinas in northern Coahuila (both flow into the Rio Grande at today's Falcon Reservoir)—they entered "a desert of very rugged mountains, so arid that there was no game." New guides joined them at this point, people so afraid of them that they did not speak or raise their eyes. They led them 150 miles across the barren, rocky landscape. Everyone suffered great hunger. At last, the four travelers found themselves once again at the Rio Grande.

Ever since turning inland in Tamaulipas, the travelers had been walking more or less parallel to the river, 50 to 100 miles south of it, and they had covered about 450 miles. Now they had come to the Big Bend of the Rio Grande. They waded up to their chests again as they crossed the river into what is now Texas's Big Bend National Park. Their exhausted guides brought them to a plain where people met them with a welcome feast of piñon nuts.

The travelers decided it was time to turn west. With summer over, they needed to get somewhere before winter. But their new guides balked at the Spaniards' request to lead them "toward the sunset" because their foes lived there.

In the end, two women, one of them a captive, went to negotiate a truce with the enemies to the west. While the rest waited for their return, many of the Indians fell sick, eight of them so sick they died. Convinced that the Spaniards and Estevanico had caused the illness out of anger, the Indians promised to take the four men wherever they wished. The

One of the most scenic areas Cabeza de Vaca passed through is the rugged hills and canyons of what later became Big Bend National Park along the Rio Grande in southwestern Texas.

Spaniards, for their part, were terrified that all the Indians might die or that they might desert them. As much as they had learned about living off the land, they could not hope to travel without support. They prayed to God for help, and the sick began to get well.

The women returned with news that most of the enemy were away hunting bison, or "cows," as Cabeza de Vaca called them. All who were well enough led the four travelers westward through the craggy peaks of the Chisos Mountains. After three days, they reached the Rio Grande again. Across the river, they could see the Río Conchos flowing out of the western range of the Sierra Madre. They had reached what is now Presidio, Texas.

José Cisneros, a Mexico-born artist who became a leading historical illustrator of the southwestern United States, shows Cabeza de Vaca and his traveling companions along the Rio Grande in the Big Bend area.

The captive woman brought them into her village, where they saw real houses of sun-baked mud, known to the Spanish as adobe, and gardens of beans and squash. Their greatest excitement was seeing corn for the first time since they had left the coast of Florida. These people did not grow corn, however, because the soil was too dry. They had bartered for the corn they had.

In the village, the Spanish learned that to continue west toward corn-growing areas they would have to follow the river still farther to the northwest for seventeen days through territory where little food could be found. Their hosts said that the people who lived there were their enemies, but they assured the men that these people would be friendly to them.

For two days, the four men pondered what to do. Meanwhile, they enjoyed stews of squash and beans that the villagers prepared for them in a way that Cabeza de Vaca found "new and strange." He described it in detail: "They have no pots. In order to cook their food they fill a medium-sized gourd with water and place stones that are easily heated into a fire. When they are hot to the point of scorching they take them out with wooden tongs, and thrust them into the water in the gourd, until it boils. As soon as it boils they put what they want to cook into it, always taking out the stones as they cool off and throwing in hot ones to keep the water boiling steadily in order to cook whatever they wish."

Cabeza de Vaca was the first European to describe North American bison. Based on his account and those of later explorers, French historian André Thevet (1502–1590) included bison in a book about American flora and fauna published in Paris in 1558. This woodcut of a bison by Jean Cousin accompanied Thevet's description of the animal.

Satisfied by their meals among the "Indians of the Cows" (the name Cabeza de Vaca gave them), the four men decided that they could face seventeen days eating only a handful of deer suet a day, which they could easily carry with them. "We were always sure," Cabeza de Vaca wrote, "that by going toward sunset we should reach our desired goal."

After seventeen hungry days, they crossed the river once more. They were probably somewhere near today's bridge from El Paso, Texas, to Ciudad Juárez, Chihuahua. For seventeen more days, they hiked through the highland deserts of Chihuahua toward the setting sun. Food was still scarce.

A modern artist envisions Cabeza de Vaca with his companions looking out over a cultivated valley, perhaps in Sonora, Mexico, as his journey nears its end.

One day they met people who ate nothing but dried grasses ground to a powder for four months of the year, "and since we passed by just at that time, we had to eat it as well."

At last, they arrived at a town with adobe houses and plenty of harvested corn. The people there gave them great quantities of cornmeal as well as squash, beans, and cotton blankets, and the four travelers as usual gave these gifts to the hardy souls who had come with them on their arduous trek. The Indians of the Cows trudged home happily carrying their loot.

Thanking God for bringing them to such a bountiful land, the Spaniards and Estevanico began a new stage in their long journey. Their one-hundred league route (about three hundred miles) across Chihuahua and Sonora was not a straight path. To thread their way over the Sierra Madre Occidental, they had to zigzag north and south along river valleys to find passes leading west.

Archaeologists refer to the civilization that then flourished in this region of northwestern Mexico as Sonora River Culture. For two hundred years before Spaniards came to the area, people were building adobe houses on stone foundations and planting corn, beans, squash, and cotton in the river valleys. Sonoran weavers produced fine cloth that traders carried as far north as the Pueblo Indians of southwestern United States and as far south as the Aztec capital in present-day Mexico City.

The "Corn Trail," as Cabeza de Vaca called it, led them through villages every two or three days. Besides food, people offered them deer hides, cotton blankets, coral beads from the Pacific Ocean, and turquoises from what is now the southwestern United States. At one stop, they gave Dorantes five arrowheads made of turquoises of such a lustrous green

This illustration from the Florentine Codex, an encyclopedia of Aztec life written around 1570, shows two Native Americans at work in their maize (corn) crop. On his journey, Cabeza de Vaca found corn-growing regions in Florida and Sonora, Mexico.

that Cabeza de Vaca thought they were emeralds. Women in the region dressed in long elegant deerskin skirts, cotton shirts laced with leather thongs, and deerskin shoes.

As before, people crowded around them to be blessed and escorted them from one town to the next. Taking advantage of the reverence people showed them, the four men spoke to them about God who lived in Heaven and created Heaven and Earth. They said they worshipped Him as their Lord because all good things came from Him, and they preached obedience to God's commands. "Had there been a language in which we could have made ourselves perfectly understood, we would have left them all Christians," Cabeza de Vaca wrote. They were, his report assured the Spanish king, open to conversion to Christianity.

In one of the towns, the people gave them more than six hundred hearts of deer to eat. These were split open and dried like jerky. Cabeza de Vaca called the place Corazones— "Hearts." The travelers had reached the western edge of the corn-growing area. Beyond it, a coastal plain stretched to the Gulf of California, about thirty-six miles away. The people along the coast, they were told, lived on powdered grasses and fish. So the travelers turned south in order to remain within the corn-growing region where food was abundant. It was late December 1535 or early January 1536. The four conquistadors had indeed crossed the country from one sea to the other and had learned much to report to their sovereign about the land and the people in it.

RESCUE AND BETRAYAL

A day's journey from Corazones, heavy rains stopped the travelers in their tracks. A river ahead of them rose so high that they could not cross it. During the two weeks the men waited for the floods to recede, Castillo spied a curious pendant on the neck of a native. Examining it more closely, he saw it was made of an iron belt buckle and a horseshoe nail. He must have recognized immediately that these items were Spanish made.

The four men eagerly quizzed the man. Once they got past the claim that the articles came from the sky, they learned that some men with beards like theirs had arrived (also from the sky) with horses, lances, and swords and had speared and killed two Indians. Where are they now? the four wanted to know. They had gone to the sea, the people explained, and entered the water "and that afterwards they saw them on top of the waves moving toward sunset."

86

Joyful to know they must be close to Spanish-held territory, Cabeza de Vaca and his companions set out as soon as the waters ebbed. As they traveled, however, they saw great devastation all around. Houses stood empty. Weeds flourished in burned-out fields. The few people they saw were thin and pale, having survived on tree bark and roots. Yet they offered the four travelers cotton blankets as they told how marauding Spaniards had destroyed and burned their villages and carried off men, women, and children.

Hearing their plight, Cabeza de Vaca was astonished that these poor people did not treat them badly in retaliation for what their countrymen had done. "It clearly shows," Cabeza de Vaca later reported to the king, "how, in order to bring those people to Christianity and obedience unto Your Imperial Majesty, they should be well treated, and not otherwise."

He promised the people that he would tell the Spaniards "not to kill Indians or make slaves of them nor take them away from their homelands, or do any other harm."

The people they met took them up a steep trail into mountains where those who escaped the Spanish slave hunters were hiding. Like the Canarians who had fled Cabeza de Vaca's grandfather, the Indians had taken refuge in rugged heights. As they walked along, they saw signs of recent campfires. Runners sent to scout the area reported seeing Spaniards with Indians in chains. Frightened, the people wanted to flee higher into the sierra, but Cabeza de Vaca assured them that they would come to no harm.

The next morning, Cabeza de Vaca left with Estevanico and eleven guides. Walking quickly, they covered over thirty miles the first day and passed three places where the slavers had camped overnight. The following day, Cabeza de Vaca's group came upon four horsemen.

The Spaniards stared speechless at the bearded man "in such strange attire and in the company of Indians." Cabeza de Vaca broke the stunned silence by ordering them to take him to their captain.

At the Spanish camp, Cabeza de Vaca learned what was going on. Nuño de Guzmán, who was governor of Pánuco when the Narváez expedition began, had in 1531 received the title of governor of Nueva Galicia, with license to explore, conquer, and settle northwestern Mexico. Two years later, Guzmán's men sailed north along the eastern shore of the Gulf of California as far as the Yaqui River, which some scholars think is the same river, farther upstream, that flowed past Corazones and delayed the travelers by flooding. These explorers were very likely the bearded men "from the sky" who had killed two Indians and who were the source of the iron belt buckle and horseshoe nail that Castillo had noticed.

After establishing several towns farther south, Guzmán granted slaving licenses to captains who had aided his conquests. Among them was Diego de Alcaraz. Shortly before the four survivors of the Narváez expedition arrived in the area, Alcaraz had sailed to the mouth of the Sinaloa River and led armed horsemen and enslaved natives from other parts of Mexico inland to capture local Indians. These were the men Cabeza de Vaca now faced.

Alcaraz told Cabeza de Vaca that he was himself in distress. He had captured no Indians in the area, he said, and his own men and the slaves he had brought with him were near starvation, for they had been unable to find food. Now it was up to Cabeza de Vaca to rescue his countrymen. He sent Estevanico with three horsemen and fifty of Alcaraz's slaves to fetch Dorantes and Castillo. Six hundred Indians returned

This engraving (from de Bry's 1594 edition of Girolamo Benzoni's Historia dei Nuovo Mondo, *or "History of the New World," shows a conquistador leading four thousand captive Native Americans to work as slaves. Benzoni, an Italian trader, spent many years (1541-1556) in Spanish America.*

with them, and six hundred more arrived later with pots of corn they had buried to hide from the slavers.

Full stomachs did not resolve the differences in outlook between Cabeza de Vaca and Diego de Alcaraz. The two men argued bitterly about Alcaraz's right to enslave the Indians. The laws of Spain stated that "rebellious" Indians could be enslaved, but the interpretation of "rebellious" left a large legal loophole for slavers to march through. Committees of churchmen, judicial courts, and royal representatives tried to stop conquistadors from twisting the law to suit their purposes, but they usually caught up with them only after the fact. Within a year, Nuño de Guzmán would be hailed into court for mistreating Indians. The licenses he gave to slavers would be one of the charges against him.

To Diego de Alcaraz, Indians were his reward for military service in a demanding environment. He wanted them to work his newly won land so that he could make the fortune he had risked his life coming to America to achieve. To Cabeza de Vaca, Indians were people. The "Corn People," the "Indians of the Cows," and all of the Native Americans who made his journey across the continent possible were, in his view, intelligent human beings and valuable allies for the Spanish colonies—in fact, essential to their success.

The Indians who had befriended Cabeza de Vaca hesitated to leave, but Cabeza de Vaca urged them to return to their villages and plant their crops. He loaded the Spaniards down with bison hides and other gifts to compensate them for not taking slaves.

Meanwhile, Alcaraz had his interpreter tell the local inhabitants that he and his men were the lords of the land, not Cabeza de Vaca and the three others. Indians, he said, should obey and serve Alcaraz, not the hapless refugees. But the people answered that the slavers lied, "for we had come from the sunrise, while they had come from where the sun sets; that we cured the sick, while they had killed those who were healthy; that we went naked and barefoot, whereas they wore clothes and went on horseback and carried lances. Also we asked for nothing, but gave away all we were presented with, while they had no other aim than to steal what they could, and never gave anything to anybody. In short, they recalled all our deeds, and praised them highly, contrasting them with the conduct of the others."

In the end, Alcaraz agreed to protect the Indians and

Cabeza de Vaca convinced them to return to their villages in peace. Alcaraz offered the four survivors an escort to San Miguel de Culiacán, then the northernmost Spanish outpost on the west coast of America. But Alcaraz had no intention of keeping his word. He sent them by a devious route through forests and uninhabited land so as to cut them off from any communication with native peoples. For two days, they traveled without water, expecting to die of thirst. Meanwhile, Alcaraz and the rest of his men pursued and captured the people who had saved them with their hidden corn.

"Do you not believe, Christian reader," Oviedo wrote in his chronicle, "that one should ponder on the difference between the ways and practices of the Spaniards that were in that land and that of the four pilgrims: the former making slaves and attacking, as told above, and the latter curing the sick and working miracles?"

RETURN TO SPAIN

After two days on the desert detour, the hot, thirsty hikers stopped at one of the few indigenous villages still remaining along the Culiacán River, a few miles north of San Miguel. The Spanish governor of Culiacán Province, Melchior Díaz, hurried out from San Miguel to greet them. Deeply moved to see the four men who so long ago had been given up for dead, Díaz praised God for their safe return and listened with grief and anger to their account of how Alcaraz had treated them.

Díaz told them how the town of San Miguel, founded five years earlier by ninety-six Spanish settlers, had fallen on hard times. Instead of planting crops, the settlers had expected the local people to supply their needs. But the people, unwilling to submit to enforced labor, had burned their homes and fled. The fertile, well-populated valley, where corn, beans, peppers, and cotton once flourished, had become a thorny scrubland. Even the discovery of silver mines in the area had not improved life much for the settlers.

Díaz begged the men to stay and help him to restore the wasted land. The Indians trust you, he said, "send for them and urge them, in the name of God and of [His] Majesty, to return to the plain and cultivate the soil again."

Assured that Díaz would enforce the antislavery laws, the four survivors sent a group of Indians with one of the gourds to ask the people in the sierras to come speak with them. A week later, three chiefs and fifteen other men arrived. Using an interpreter and the phrasing of the first part of the requerimiento, Melchior Díaz promised to look upon all the Indians as brothers and treat them all well if they would believe in God and serve Him. To this the chiefs, through the interpreter, replied "that they would be very good Christians and serve God."

The Spaniards asked the Indians to rebuild their former homes and settle the land again. Among their houses, they should build one to God and place a cross on it. The children of the chiefs were then baptized, and Díaz "pledged himself before God not to make a raid or allow one to be made or to capture slaves from the people and in the country we had set at peace again." This "peaceful conquest" was so successful that when Alcaraz and his slaving party returned two weeks later, they were amazed to find the deserted villages repopulated. The Indians had come out to greet him carrying crosses, Alcaraz told Díaz, and had taken him into their houses and given him food and even a place to sleep.

After this satisfying victory, Cabeza de Vaca and his companions set out for Compostela, where Nuño de Guzmán, the governor of Nueva Galicia, had his capital. It was a very different kind of journey. For now they rode horseback, and instead of friendly Indian guides, twenty armed horsemen escorted them, ready to defend the convoy from Indian attack. Along the way, six more Spaniards joined the group, leading five hundred Indian captives in iron yokes and chains.

Guzmán welcomed them, but Cabeza de Vaca must have found it hard to accept the hospitality of a man so notorious for mistreating Native Americans. Cabeza de Vaca only wrote that he could not bear to wear the clothing the governor so kindly gave him nor could he sleep anywhere but on the bare floor. Perhaps it was the habit of eight long years without European-style clothing or beds. Or maybe it was horror at the thought of becoming like one of them.

Spanish invaders led by Captain Nuño de Guzmán conquered the Purépecha Indians of Michoacán in 1530. This scene is based on a sixteenth-century Aztec drawing of the armed conflict.

Ten or twelve days later—by now it was June—the men left for Mexico City. Curious to see men who had miraculously survived shipwreck and had walked thousands of miles through uncharted lands—where no Europeans had gone before—colonists poured out of towns along the way. The travelers arrived July 23, just in time for public celebrations on Saint James Day two days later.

Few Spanish towns celebrated holidays as splendidly as Mexico City did in the 1500s. Crowds packed the principal plaza to see dramatic presentations, rodeo stunts, bullfights, and *juegos de cañas*—a kind of joust in which teams of horsemen, riding at full gallop, hurl wooden lances at one another. On Saint James Day 1536, as an added attraction, the four survivors of the Narváez expedition appeared in their skimpy deerskins, "just as they had arrived from the land of Florida" one witness said. Church bells rang in commemoration of their deliverance.

Among the people who turned out to see the heroes of the day was Alonso de Barrera, one of the hundred members of the Narváez expedition who remained on the ships when Narváez marched inland, his mind dazzled with rumors of Apalache gold. After a year of searching for their companions, the expedition members gave them up for dead. Barrera later settled in Mexico City where he worked as a tailor. He met with the survivors and heard about their many hardships.

The viceroy, Antonio de Mendoza, had only recently arrived in New Spain to curb the power of Hernán Cortés and integrate the colony more fully into the legal jurisdiction of the Spanish king. The viceroy quizzed the four survivors about exploitable resources and hinted that their services would be most welcome on future expeditions north.

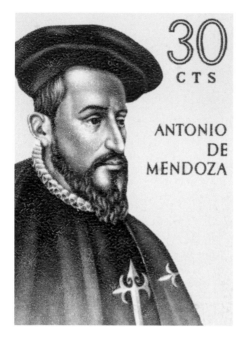

This Spanish stamp commemorates Antonio de Mendoza (1490-1552), the first Spanish viceroy in America. Mendoza represented the Spanish king in New Spain (modern Mexico) from 1535 to 1550. He later served briefly as viceroy of Peru (1551-1552).

That summer Cabeza de Vaca, Castillo, and Dorantes wrote an account of the expedition. As the only surviving officials, they were responsible for explaining everything that had occurred. Their joint report does not survive, but Oviedo used a copy of it to write his history of the expedition.

Meanwhile, they caught up on news about what happened while they were away. The most talked-about event was surely the discovery and conquest of the Inca Empire in Peru in the early 1530s. Cabeza de Vaca would have heard about the quantities of gold and silver shipped to Spain. He probably also heard of the massacres, torture, and treachery that Francisco Pizarro and Diego de Almagro committed to seize control of the treasures, the land, and the people.

By September, Cabeza de Vaca was eager to return to Spain. He got as far as Veracruz on the Gulf coast of Mexico, but as he waited for his ship to load, a hurricane blew in and capsized it. Reluctantly, he returned to Mexico City for the winter. In April he was luckier. Even then two other ships in the convoy did not make it even as far as Havana. In early July, French privateers—pirates licensed by the French king to prey on Spanish shipping—pursued Cabeza de Vaca's ship as it sailed alone near the Azores, Portuguese Islands about seven hundred miles from the coast. After a narrow escape, the ship stopped at Terceira in the Azores to wait for other Spanish and Portuguese ships to form a convoy for the rest of the voyage.

The four-month journey across the Atlantic gave Cabeza de Vaca plenty of time to plan for the future. He was in his early fifties and had a wife and a home in Spain, but his heart was not ready to settle down to the life of a caballero of Jerez, sitting on the town council as his father had. Cabeza de Vaca must have thought again and again of Narváez's poor decisions and of how differently he would have done everything if he had been the leader of the expedition.

The Incas of Peru valued gold for its beauty. They used gold not as money but to make ornaments and ceremonial objects such as this image of their sun god. Most of these works of religious art were melted down by the conquistadors and shaped into ingots (bars) for easy transport and exchange.

How much better prepared he was now, knowing what he had learned about the land and the people, about himself and human nature, to lead men into new lands claimed by Spain. He had probably always been self assured, yet the ordeal in North America had increased both his self-confidence and his faith in God. That was why he was in a hurry to get to Spain: to petition King Charles for the right to colonize the lands earlier assigned to Narváez.

The large flotilla reached the mouth of the Tagus River in Portugal in early August 1537. River pilots who steered ships up the Tagus to Lisbon passed along recent news to passengers long at sea. It is likely that from them Cabeza de Vaca heard a report that dashed his hopes of replacing Narváez. Back in April, just ten days after he sailed from Veracruz, the Spanish king had appointed Hernando de Soto to lead a new expedition to Florida.

A NEW ASSIGNMENT

If Cabeza de Vaca was disappointed to learn that De Soto had won the appointment he hoped for, he was not discouraged. The Indies, he knew, were vast, and Spanish interest in finding and colonizing new lands had clearly soared after the amazing discovery of Inca wealth in Peru. King Charles was certain to want to put Cabeza de Vaca's knowledge and skills to work somewhere in the New World.

Exploration and conquest were vital to the king's agenda. Charles envisioned himself as the leader of a Europe united into a Christian superpower. That ambition had to overcome the opposition of France. He also faced dissension within the Holy Roman Empire. The Reformation, Martin Luther's Protestant revolt against Roman Catholicism, was beginning to split Europe into religious factions. Many German princes, who were in theory Charles's allies, supported Luther. Charles also had to protect his possessions in Austria and Hungary from the Islamic Ottoman Empire to the east and defend Spanish shipping in the Mediterranean and the Atlantic from North African pirates. To pay troops on so many fronts, Charles constantly needed money. Gold and silver arriving from the Americas helped relieve his pinched treasury.

As he traveled upriver, Cabeza de Vaca would also have heard other news from the Indies. Among the ships in the convoy from Terceira was one that had sailed from a struggling Spanish colony on the Río de la Plata in South America. The governor of the colony, Don Pedro de Mendoza, had been aboard, but before arriving in Europe, he died and was buried at sea.

Mendoza's comptroller, Felipe de Cáceres, who crossed the Atlantic with him, immediately rushed off to the Spanish

This marble bas-relief (relief sculpture) of a conquistador appears on a fountain in Buenos Aires, Argentina. When the monument was built in 1937, its location was thought to have been where the Spanish, led by Don Pedro de Mendoza, first settled in the area in 1536.

court in Valladolid to report on conditions in his beleaguered colony. Cabeza de Vaca heard much about Mendoza, whose unfortunate story competed for attention with that of his own miraculous return.

Río de la Plata, a broad channel between present-day Uruguay and Argentina, first caught the attention of Portuguese explorers in 1514. The following year, the Spanish king Ferdinand sent his chief pilot, Juan Díaz de Solís, to survey the area. Solís soon determined that the wide inlet was not a strait leading to the Pacific Ocean, as everyone hoped, but the estuary (tidal mouth) of two rivers, the Uruguay and the Paraná. While exploring the north shore, Solís and a few companions were attacked and killed by Indians. Watching in horror from the ships, the other expedition members saw the Indians eat the slain Spaniards.

As Solís's three ships sailed back to Spain, one ran aground off the coast of Brazil. The ship's captain, the Portuguese navigator Alejo García, and other survivors lived among the local Guaraní Indians for several years. In 1524 they joined a raid, led by Guaranís, on wealthy Inca towns on the southeastern edge of the Inca Empire. Loaded with gold and silver treasures, the looters were returning to the Atlantic coast, when Guaycurú Indians ambushed them and stole all their treasure. García was killed, but some of the Europeans reached the coast with reports of a fabulously rich kingdom in the interior of South America.

When the news reached Spain, the river's name quickly changed from Río de Solís to Río de la Plata—"River of Silver." Later efforts to retrace García's route failed to find anything but hostile cannibals and more rumors of treasure.

Mendoza's ill-fated expedition was an ambitious effort to tap that storied wealth. In August 1535, as Cabeza de Vaca and his companions were leaving the Avavares in Mexico, Mendoza sailed across the Atlantic with fourteen ships carrying more than twelve hundred men, many accompanied by their wives. His mission was to establish Spanish towns and forts on the Río de la Plata to prevent any Portuguese claim to the area, as it lay close to the line between Spanish and Portuguese territory established in the treaty of 1494.

The settlers built Nuestra Señora Santa María de los Buenos Aires—"Our Lady Saint Mary of Favorable Winds"— on the south bank of Río de la Plata. Local Querandí Indians at first welcomed them with fish and meat. But when the settlers tried to force the Indians to give them food, they responded with flint-tipped arrows and deftly hurled bolas— stones with strings attached—that tripped up Spanish horses and flung Spanish caballeros to their deaths.

This nineteenth-century painting shows South American Indians using bolas to trip fleeing guanacos. The horses they are riding would be descendants of those brought to the continent by the Spanish.

The colonists encircled their homes with a stockade and a ditch for protection. Unable to leave their fort to fish or farm, they were soon starving. "The hunger was so great," one of the women wrote later, "that within three months one thousand died." Another account reported that when three Spaniards were hung on the gallows as punishment for killing a horse for food, hungry settlers hacked off pieces of the hanged men and took them home to eat.

Mendoza himself was seriously ill with syphilis and decided to return to Spain for help. Before leaving, he appointed his chief constable Juan de Ayolas to rule in his absence.

While Spain absorbed the appalling stories from South America, Cabeza de Vaca headed home to Jerez and his

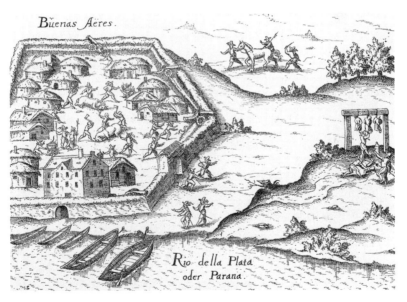

This engraving from a 1599 edition of Ulrich Schmidel's account of his twenty years in America depicts Buenos Aires during the famine of 1536. Desperate for food, the settlers are cutting pieces from the bodies of three men hanged for killing horses. The settlers are also butchering more horses.

wife, whom he had not seen in ten years. His mind, however, was very much set on winning a new assignment in the Indies. To bolster his petition, he asked his cousin Pedro Estopiñan to prepare an account of his grandfather's services to Ferdinand and Isabella as a way of showing the family's nobility and royal service.

That fall Cabeza de Vaca went to Seville to report to the House of Trade on the Narváez expedition. In November or December, he traveled to Valladolid to speak personally with King Charles. Members of the de Soto expedition were also in Valladolid, preparing to depart for North America. De Soto invited Cabeza de Vaca to come with him. Cabeza de Vaca turned him down "because he ... did not wish to go under the banner of another."

This 1791 engraving is based on a portrait of Hernando de Soto painted by José Maea. De Soto spent three years (1539-1541) searching for gold and making war on Native Americans in the southeastern United States. In 1542 he died on the banks of the Mississippi. Fewer than half of his men survived the expedition.

Cabeza de Vaca had already experienced the consequences of following the orders of a leader he disagreed with, and he probably suspected that he would not see eye-to-eye with de Soto on the subject of Native Americans. De Soto had won a name for himself fighting in Nicaragua and in Peru on two of the most brutal campaigns of the Spanish conquest. Besides, during his ten years in North America, Cabeza de Vaca had formed definite ideas about how to colonize the Indies. He wanted to lead, not follow.

For three years, Cabeza de Vaca waited. Ships sailed for Río de la Plata in the fall of 1537 with men and supplies. De Soto departed the following April. Cabeza de Vaca, meanwhile, poured his heart into writing the *Relación*, addressed to the king but intended also for publication. As its title indicates, the *Relación*—"the Account"—was Cabeza de Vaca's report as a royal official of his activities and of the people and places he saw. Its detailed descriptions provide the earliest written record we have of Native Americans of Texas and northern Mexico and their customs—their languages, weapons, housing, clothing, methods of hunting and cooking, sexuality, and religious beliefs and rituals. Most remarkable, almost all of these fascinating portrayals are objective and nonjudgmental.

Cabeza de Vaca also planned the *Relación* to show the king his qualifications as a leader. In particular, he emphasized his conviction that American Indians could be won over to Spanish rule through Christian teaching, not force.

Feelings ran high in Spain concerning the goals and methods of conquest. News of atrocities in the Americas horrified many Spaniards. Many clergymen preached against the enslavement of Indians. Bartolomé de las Casas continued his outspoken defense of Native

American rights. In the 1530s, Las Casas's tract *The Only Method of Attracting All People to the True Faith* presented his vision of humane and peaceful conquest to clergy and statesmen. Even the pope joined the debate by issuing a bull (decree) in 1537 declaring that American native peoples are rational beings, not brute animals, and "are by no means to be deprived of their liberty or the possession of their property, even though they be outside the faith of Jesus Christ."

Opponents, among them King Charles's chaplain, Juan Ginés de Sepúlveda, argued that the native peoples had to be subdued by force because they were incapable of reason and self-rule. Sepúlveda pointed to Aztec idolatry (the worship of a physical object as a god) and human sacrifice as evidence of Indian inferiority.

Without commenting directly on the debates raging around him, Cabeza de Vaca wrote in the *Relación* that Native Americans were not beasts or savages but people. "In the 2,000 leagues we traveled," he wrote as if in answer to Sepúlveda, "nowhere did we come upon either sacrifices or idolatry."

At last, on March 18, 1540, the Council of the Indies appointed Álvar Nuñez Cabeza de Vaca governor of the Río de la Plata colony and adelantado to lead an exploration over a wide, mostly uncharted area to the north and west. He was expected to invest eight thousand ducats in the enterprise for horses, supplies, arms, and munitions. Since Spain had no recent news from the colony concerning Ayolas, whom Mendoza had appointed to govern the colony in his absence, the contract specified that only if Ayolas were dead would Cabeza de Vaca become governor of the colony. Otherwise, he would be second-in-command.

Cabeza de Vaca must have thought over the situation. If he were not in charge, it might be difficult to put in action the principles he supported. But chances that Ayolas was still alive were slim. Three years had passed with no word of him. Cabeza de Vaca decided to go for it.

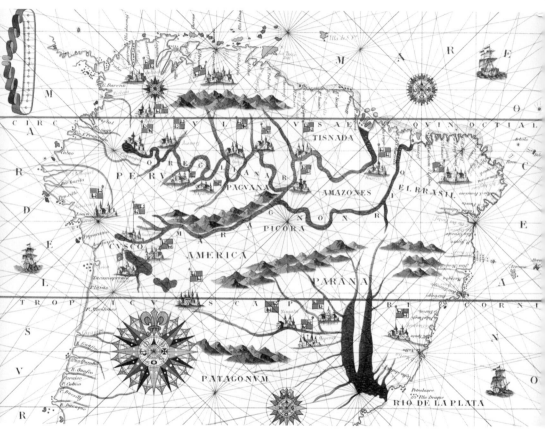

Joan Martines, a mapmaker from Majorca, made this chart of South America for an atlas printed in Messina, Sicily, in 1582. The broad estuary of Río de la Plata appears at the lower right.

BLAZING A TRAIL
TO ASUNCIÓN

The province assigned to Cabeza de Vaca, like the province assigned to Narváez fourteen years earlier, was vast and vaguely defined. It stretched from the Río de la Plata to the Pacific and included six hundred miles of Pacific coastline. Although the Río de la Plata estuary and its main tributaries had been appearing on Spanish maps for a quarter of a century, what lay to the west was anybody's guess. Cabeza de Vaca's task was to explore, conquer, and settle as much of this unknown territory as possible.

Royal decree also named Cabeza de Vaca governor of Santa Catalina (modern Santa Catarina), an island off the coast of Brazil about six hundred miles northward of Río de la Plata. The decree added that if it turned out that Ayolas were still alive, making Cabeza de Vaca lieutenant governor instead of governor of Río de la Plata, Cabeza de Vaca would still rule Santa Catalina for twelve years.

Cabeza de Vaca spent the summer of 1540 raising funds for the trip by borrowing from family and friends. He bought four ships and crammed them with provisions—eight or ten cows for milk and meat on the journey, dried ship's biscuits, flour, salted fish and meat, beans and chickpeas, rice, salt, cheeses, wine, oil, vinegar, medicines, and barrels of water. Other cargo included knives, fishhooks, mirrors, scissors, red caps, shirts, and shawls to trade with the local people; and clothing, bales of wool and linen cloth, iron tools and nails, wax, soap, and books for life in the distant colony. He also purchased forty-eight horses.

Cabeza de Vaca recruited nine priests and friars and four hundred well-trained men-at-arms as expedition members. He supplied the clergy with vestments, chalices and other ritual dishes, communion wafers, and wine, and the military with armor and either a crossbow or a harquebus—a heavy musket usually fired from a support.

The shooter of the harquebus ignited gunpowder that propelled a ball, or bullet, out of the gun. The gun was usually fired from a support.

A number of friends and relations from Jerez de la Frontera signed on, including his cousin Pedro Estopiñan and the son of one of his sisters. A few women, some artisans, four African slaves, and two Native Americans, one from Mexico, were among the people traveling with him.

Of the four men chosen to look after the king's interests, the three higher-ranked officials—the treasurer, Garci Venegas; the comptroller, Felipe de Cáceres; and the inspector, Alonso Cabrera—were holdovers from Mendoza's expedition. The tax agent was Pedro Dorantes (apparently no relation of Cabeza de Vaca's fellow survivor of the Narváez disaster, Andrés Dorantes). Only Cáceres and Dorantes traveled from Spain with Cabeza de Vaca. The other two were already in South America.

By the end of September, all was ready. But the crossing was poorly timed. After leaving Seville and passing inspection at Sanlúcar de Barrameda at the mouth of the Guadalquivir, the three ships sailed out into a gale that forced them to take shelter in Cádiz harbor until December. In the Canaries, they spent another three weeks waiting for favorable winds. Then the largest ship developed leaks, forcing the flotilla to stop in the Cape Verde islands for repairs.

From Cape Verde, they sailed south along the African coast until, with freshwater running low, Cabeza de Vaca gave orders to head west to look for land. A rooster that had been silent the entire voyage woke everyone with his crowing one morning and saved the ships from foundering on sharp rocks off the coast of Brazil. "We all thought it a miracle of God for us," Cabeza de Vaca's secretary Pedro Hernández wrote later.

The expedition finally reached Santa Catalina on March 29, 1541, six months after leaving Seville. Everyone gratefully disembarked, glad to feel solid earth beneath their feet.

Explorations of
Cabeza de Vaca in South America
1541 to 1544

OREJONES

Los Reyes •

GUAYCURÚS

BOLIVIA

GUARANÍS

Río Paraguay

Río Paraná

BRAZIL

route of
Cabeza de Vaca
to Asunción

Miles
0   50   100 150 200

0   100   200   300
Kilometers

Asunción •
AGAZ

Iguazú
Falls

VERA PROVINCE

Río Iguazú

PARAGUAY

ARGENTINA

Río Uruguay

Río Paraná

URUGUAY

Buenos
Aires •

Río de la Plata

N

ATLANTIC OCEAN
(SOUTH SEA)

SANTA
CATALINA ISLAND
(SANTA
CATARINA ISLAND)

SOUTH
AMERICA

PERU

BRAZIL

BOLIVIA

PARAGUAY

ARGENTINA

URUGUAY

Area
of map

Only twenty-six horses survived the ordeal of the voyage.
Guaranís living on the island had long ago grown used to
European ships calling at Santa Catalina for freshwater, fire-
wood, and other provisions and probably paid no attention to
the possession ceremony in which Cabeza de Vaca claimed
Santa Catalina for Spain.

In May, Cabeza de Vaca sent Felipe de Cáceres to Buenos
Aires to let the colony know that he would soon be on his way.
Stormy weather, however, prevented the ship from entering

Río de la Plata, and it returned to Santa Catalina. Soon afterward, a boat from Buenos Aires arrived at the island with nine Europeans. These refugees told Cabeza de Vaca what had occurred in the colony since Mendoza left in 1537.

While Mendoza's deputy Ayolas was on the Upper Paraguay River looking for gold, they said, he appointed Captain Domingo Martínez de Irala to guard the riverboats while he marched inland. When Ayolas returned with Indians in pursuit, the boats were gone, leaving Ayolas with no means of escape. The refugees blamed Irala for Ayolas's death.

Many colonists blamed Domingo Martinez de Irala for the death of governor Juan de Ayolas after Irala had abandoned Ayola's riverboats on an expedition. In this engraving de Bry shows Irala executing two Native Americans as a punishment for killing Ayolas.

A bitter struggle for leadership arose in the colony. The stronger faction elected Irala governor. Irala moved most of the colony to Asunción, a new town on a bluff overlooking the Paraguay River, about 750 miles up the Paraná and Paraguay rivers, leaving only eighty settlers in Buenos Aires. The nine refugees had fled because they were fed up with Indian attacks, food shortages, and squabbling colonists.

Studying the situation, Cabeza de Vaca decided to divide his expedition. He would lead the majority of the men and supplies overland to Asunción, which lies about six hundred miles west northwest of Santa Catalina as the crow flies (Cabeza de Vaca's actual route was twice as long). Meanwhile, the ships could carry everyone else to Buenos Aires and wait there for future orders. Felipe de Cáceres argued that everyone should go first to Buenos Aires, but Cabeza de Vaca overruled him, saying that the overland trek would get needed supplies to Asunción quicker than sailing to Buenos Aires first and then towing boats upstream. Besides, he admitted, his purpose was "as much to discover as to aid [the colony]."

Showing more caution than Narváez did in Florida, he sent Pedro Dorantes with one hundred armed men to make certain that an overland route was possible. Three and a half months later, Dorantes reported that although the first part over mountains and deserted land was rough going, beyond that lay a fertile plain. Friendly Guaranís assured him it was the best route inland.

On November 2, 1541, Cabeza de Vaca, 250 harquebusiers and crossbowmen, local guides, and the twenty-six horses marched into southeastern Brazil. For nineteen days, they struggled through dense tropical forests and over steep mountains. Just as they were running out of food, they came to the plain Dorantes spoke of. Welcoming Guaranís offered them corn cakes and roasted ducks to eat.

For several weeks, the Spaniards progressed from village to village. Everywhere they went, people brought them food—corn, cassava, potatoes, peanuts, honey, fish, ducks, and geese. Cabeza de Vaca paid for the provisions with Spanish knives, scissors, mirrors, and other trade goods. To avoid any misunderstandings, he kept his men-at-arms out of the villages and forbade them to barter with the Indians.

As news of the Spaniards spread, villagers from miles around came out to meet them—just as Indians in Sonora had come to see the four castaways years earlier. Women and children watched the parade of strangely dressed, bearded white men, "a thing that had never before been seen in the land." Afraid of the horses, the people left treats of duck meat and honey especially for them on the pathway.

Noting the "large plains, forests, many rivers, streams and rivulets, with abundance of good drinking water," Cabeza de Vaca remarked that even with no sign of precious metals, the land was valuable, for it was "very suitable for cultivation and stock-rearing." On November 29, he performed a ceremony taking possession of this "newly discovered land" for the Spanish Crown, naming it Vera to honor his grandfather.

In early December, the expedition met Miguel, a baptized Guaraní from Santa Catalina, who was on his way home from Asunción. Miguel offered to turn around and show the Spaniards the route. Cabeza de Vaca gladly accepted and sent his other guides back to Santa Catalina with many gifts.

The landscape changed. Evergreen forests, steeper mountains, and then marshy lowlands overgrown with sharp-pointed reeds slowed their progress. The men cut through thickets and built bridges to cross rivers and dangerous swamps. Forests "so thick that the sky cannot be seen over-head" and trees so large that four men could not join hands around their trunks impressed the Spaniards.

Distances between Guaraní villages increased, and food became scarce. Miguel showed the Spaniards how to find drinking water in the hollows of bamboolike reeds and finger-sized larvae to fry for food.

In early January 1542, some Spaniards fell ill. Rather than wait for them to recover, Cabeza de Vaca gave the local peo-ple many presents to care for them and left them behind. He also sent two Indians ahead to Asunción to ask the Spaniards to send two riverboats to meet them where the Iguazú River empties into the Paraná, so that any march-weary troops could complete their journey by water.

On January 31, they reached the Iguazú River. Their guides warned them that the Guaranís along the river were enemies and had slain a Portuguese explorer. To be safe, Cabeza de Vaca split his troops, sending the majority along the river with the horses and taking eighty armed men himself in canoes.

As they paddled downstream, the men heard the roar of approaching falls and saw spray rising high up into the air ahead. They quickly scrambled to the bank and pulled their craft out of the water. Lugging the heavy canoes through dense underbrush along the bank, they passed the dramatic sight of the now famous Iguazú Falls. Cabeza de Vaca must have been too intent on the possible dangers to stop and admire them, for he says nothing of their natural beauty.

When they reached the place where the Iguazú empties into the Paraná and the men in the canoes joined those who had walked overland, they met a large force of Guaranís wearing brightly colored paint and feathers and holding bows and arrows ready for battle. Undaunted, Cabeza de Vaca

The Iguazú Falls on the border of Brazil and Argentina are a system of waterfalls spread over almost two miles. Iguazú, in the Guaraní language, means "big water." The tallest of the falls is 270 feet.

defused the standoff by offering gifts. Pleased with their presents, the Indians put aside their weapons and helped the Spaniards cross the swift whirlpools of the river junction.

The two riverboats Cabeza de Vaca requested had not arrived. After claiming the Paraná River for Spain, Cabeza de Vaca loaded the canoes with all those too sick or worn out to walk, along with fifty crossbowmen and harquebusiers to defend them. A Guaraní headman agreed to show them the way to a friendly village downstream where they could await the riverboats in greater comfort.

Asunción was now nine days' walk away. Everyone's spirits rose at the thought that the long trek was almost done. Marshes and rivers still had to be crossed, but natives brought food and guided their way. A Spaniard even came out several days' walk from Asunción to greet them. More and more of the Guaranís they met spoke Spanish. "Along the route they entered into conversation with us," Pedro Hernández wrote later, "and were as cordial and familiar as though they were our own countrymen, born and bred in Spain."

At nine in the morning on March 11, Cabeza de Vaca arrived in Asunción. In four months, he had led an army of 250 men from the coast of Brazil to the central plains of South America, befriended native peoples, and claimed a broad swath of southern Brazil and Paraguay for Spain—all without firing a shot. He had lost only three men in the process. One Spaniard drowned crossing the Paraná, one man died of an unknown illness, and a jaguar felled the third. Unlike most Spanish conquistadors, Cabeza de Vaca did not ride horseback on this arduous journey. "I always walked on foot and barefoot," he wrote later, "to encourage the people so that they did not become demoralized."

All but one of the sick men left in Guaraní care recovered and walked to Asunción several weeks later, and Cabeza de Vaca sent riverboats to collect those who went down the Paraná in canoes. It was a difficult but successful and peaceful march, a remarkable achievement probably comparable in the history of the Spanish conquest only to his own longer and equally barefoot walk from the east coast of Texas to the west coast of Mexico.

HUMANE
CONQUISTADOR

When Cabeza de Vaca walked into Asunción, a banner announcing a new entrada to search for gold waved in the river breezes in front of the adobe and wood fort. Eager explorers were caulking newly built riverboats, stocking up on provisions, and sharpening their swords. Irala was impatient to depart during the three-month window of opportunity when autumn winds favored upriver sailing. He had been too busy preparing to go to send the riverboats Cabeza de Vaca had requested, and now he hoped the new governor's arrival would not delay his plans.

After Irala and the royal officials greeted Cabeza de Vaca in a formal ceremony, however, the first item of business was not Irala's entrada. The year before, while Cabeza de Vaca was on Santa Catalina, Irala had evacuated the few soldiers and settlers still at the fort in Buenos Aires and brought them all to Asunción. Some said Irala had done this to cut off communications with Spain so that he could run the colony however he pleased. Irala defended his choice, saying it was better to unite the struggling colony where food was plentiful, Indians were friendly, and the rumored sources of gold and silver were closer.

Cabeza de Vaca disagreed. A fort on the Río de la Plata was necessary for ships coming and going from Spain, he reasoned. The voyage from Europe was long enough without ships having to travel three more months up rivers to reach Asunción. Travelers needed a safe place to stop for water and provisions and to transfer from seagoing vessels to smaller riverboats called *bergantinas*, which were better suited than caravels to sail up the Paraná and Paraguay rivers.

On April 27, he dispatched two boats, well stocked with food and supplies, to Buenos Aires, where he assumed his cousin Pedro Estopiñan, the ships, and 150 colonists were waiting for further orders. In fact, the ships from Spain had arrived to find only a mound of ashes—Irala had burned the fort—and a few abandoned horses, grown wild with their unexpected freedom. Estopiñan started up the Paraná, but when he met the boats from Asunción, he turned around and went back to rebuild what Irala had destroyed.

Meanwhile, in Asunción, Irala and the men itching to prospect for gold chafed with impatience, angry that boats and supplies for their entrada had disappeared downstream. Cabeza de Vaca, however, saw other problems he wanted to address before making any expeditions.

Noticing how poor and needy many of the settlers were, he gave them shirts, trousers, and weapons. They told him their poverty was caused by Irala and the royal officials, who imposed taxes on fish, butter, honey, corn, and animal skins purchased from the Native Americans. Cabeza de Vaca abolished the taxes, to the chagrin of the tax collectors.

The Indians brought up other issues. Guaranís who lived in villages and farmed land on the east bank of the Paraguay River near Asunción had originally welcomed the Spaniards as allies, for they had many enemies among the plainsmen of the Pampas and the Gran Chaco to the south, west, and north. These plainsmen were all nomads, who carried shelters of reed mats or animal hides from place to place as they followed herds of deer or the swift-running, ostrichlike birds called rheas. They often looted Guaraní villages for food, burned Guaraní houses, and massacred villagers.

The leaders of the Guaranís paid the Spanish settlers for military protection by providing them with food, labor, and wives. Irala and other officers had dozens of Guaraní women living in their households and working in their fields, their kitchens, and their beds. This polygyny appalled the clergymen who came with Cabeza de Vaca. To them the situation was especially sinful because many women related to one another were having sexual relations with one master, a form of incest, according to Catholic moralists.

Soon after Cabeza de Vaca's arrival in Asunción, Guaraní headmen complained to him that the colonists were trading women like slaves and forcing men to work for them. In response, Cabeza de Vaca had laws posted and read aloud by the town crier. Indians were not to be sold or traded or taken from their villages. They were not to be forced to work, and they were to be paid for all work that they performed. The colonists had six days to remove related Indian women from their homes. Punishments for not complying included fines, jail, public display with one's head, feet, and hands locked in the stocks, or service on the riverboats—which included the heavy work of manning the oars or towing boats upstream.

A few days after Cabeza de Vaca announced the new laws, a Guaraní man accused a Spaniard of raping his wife. Cabeza de Vaca infuriated some settlers by allowing testimony from a Native American as evidence and sentencing the Spaniard to one hundred lashes. The survivors of Mendoza's expedition had enjoyed many liberties during their years of self-rule and resented the new governor's interference with their lives. Ulrich Schmidel, a German who came with Mendoza, said "All the officers and soldiers hated him for his perverse and rigorous carriage toward the [Europeans]."

Cabeza de Vaca, determined to be firm and fair, was careful not to overreact. He punished Spaniards leniently, his cousin later testified, and he quieted victimized Indians with gifts. No European was hanged during his governance of Río de la Plata. But it was an explosive situation.

Linked to Cabeza de Vaca's concern for Native Americans was his desire to convert them to Christianity. He gave the clergy copies of instructions from the king concerning the education of Indians and provided space and materials for a house and a church. In front of all the officers and clergy, he urged Guaraní headmen to become good Christians, giving them many gifts to gain their goodwill. He did lay down one rule. The Guaranís liked to fatten up prisoners taken in war and roast them for food. Irala had not objected to the practice, but Cabeza de Vaca, saying it was a great offense against God, forbade Guaranís to eat human flesh.

Cabeza de Vaca's first test with local resistance came from the Agaz Indians, who hunted in the plains across the river from Asunción. Soon after Cabeza de Vaca's arrival, Agaz men raided and burned Guaraní villages and fields.

Instead of retaliating, Cabeza de Vaca summoned Agaz leaders. When the chiefs said that the damage occurred because a few hot-headed youths disobeyed their elders and that the guilty had been well punished for their misdeeds, Cabeza de Vaca accepted their word and received them "as vassals of His Majesty and as friends of the Christians." He promised to treat them well and give them food so long as they left Guaranís in peace, returned any captives, allowed any Agaz Indians who had converted to Christianity to worship with the Christians, and hunted and fished only west of the Paraguay River. The Agaz headmen agreed to all the conditions, and peace was restored. Old-timers in the colony shook their heads at Cabeza de Vaca's trust.

A few months later, Guaraní leaders asked for Spanish help against Guaycurú attacks. Cabeza de Vaca called together all the officers and clergy to hear witnesses and determine whether war was justified. All agreed that the Guaycurú were "implacable enemies." Cabeza de Vaca sent an embassy to request that Guaycurús cease all attacks and submit to Spanish rule. When the Guaycurús replied with arrows, Cabeza de Vaca ordered two hundred men-at-arms and twenty horsemen to prepare for action.

On July 12, he led the troops out of Asunción. Hundreds of Guaranís in feathers and war paint joined the campaign. Marching as quietly as possible under cover of trees at the foot of wooded hills, the long line closed in on unsuspecting Guaycurús out hunting for deer. The march continued into the night. Suddenly a great noise erupted among the Guaranís. Thinking that they had been attacked, the Spaniards, who were marching with lit fuses, fired wildly into the darkness. Several Guaranís were wounded, and the rest fled into the hills. Cabeza de Vaca was himself grazed across the face by a Spanish bullet.

When the wounded Indians explained that a jaguar had caused the panic, Cabeza de Vaca rushed into the forest and reminded the frightened people that the Spanish were only on this campaign to protect and defend them. Shortly before dawn, the reunited allies surprised the Guaycurús and defeated them in a bloody battle. To reduce the carnage, Cabeza de Vaca purposely allowed many to escape. After fleeing, however, the Guaycurús, ambushed Guaranís as they returned to their villages.

While Cabeza de Vaca was away, the Agaz Indians tried to take advantage of his absence and attacked the town, only to be repelled by sentries. They then raided outlying farms and looted Guaraní villages. The officers and clergy agreed that war against the Agaz was now justified. Cabeza de Vaca sent Irala on a punitive raid.

Cabeza de Vaca, however, did not become discouraged. He put his policy of trust to the test with the Guaycurús. Bringing together all the prisoners captured in the battle, he told them that the king of Spain did not wish to enslave them. He chose one man to go to his people and offer them gifts and protection in return for peace.

Four days later, the man appeared with a large number of Guaycurús on the bank of the Paraguay across from Asunción. Cabeza de Vaca sent a boat and interpreters, and twenty headmen appeared before him squatting on one foot. Speaking for all Guaycurús, they said, "we have come to offer our submission to the King of the Spaniards."

The surrender of the warlike Guaycurús amazed both settlers and Guaranís. Cabeza de Vaca gave them Spanish goods to bind the peace, and after that, Guaycurús brought weekly gifts of barbecued venison and boar, deer and jaguar skins, and brightly dyed cloth made from teasel plants.

Soon a market developed on the bluff overlooking the river. Hundreds of Guaranís and Guaycurús came to barter in canoes piled high with fish, game, corn, cassava, and peanuts. "They sometimes collide with one another, and all the merchandise falls into the water," Pedro Hernández said of the scene. "Then the Indians to whom this happens, and those awaiting on the bank, burst into fits of laughter." Dressed in their best paint and feathers, they all "talk so loud and so much, that they cannot hear one another for the noise, and all are very gay and jolly."

The peaceful scene his secretary described must have pleased Cabeza de Vaca. His policies were yielding positive results. In late July, he sent two more bergantinas to Buenos Aires with 150 men and plenty of supplies to see that colony through the rest of the winter. He was now ready to turn his thoughts toward exploration. Eager to build on the accumulated information of dozens of unfortunate explorers who had lost their lives searching for the sources of gold and silver in the interior of South America, Cabeza de Vaca began carefully planning his own entrada. No reckless, gold-crazed rush into the unknown for him. His expedition would be a well-organized search buttressed by cautious exploration, reliable supply lines, and the generous diplomacy that had helped him safely through earlier encounters with unfamiliar people in uncharted lands.

This 1599 engraving by de Bry illustrates how indigenous peoples in Guyana made idols by melting gold panned from rivers (in background). The molten metal was piped directly into molds placed around the bottom of the pot.

THE QUEST FOR GOLD

Cabeza de Vaca had borrowed heavily to finance his expedition. Part of his investment was in trade goods, but he had had no opportunity as yet to trade them for anything but the goodwill of Indians and impoverished settlers. Finding precious metals was the only way to pay his debts. The gold and silver plaques the Guaraní headmen wore on their foreheads and chests were constant reminders of mines not too far away, reportedly somewhere northwest of Asunción.

On October 20, 1542, Cabeza de Vaca sent Irala up the Paraguay River to search for a route leading west. Three bergantinas carried about ninety Spaniards and large quantities of provisions. Many Guaranís followed in their canoes.

While Cabeza de Vaca waited for news, the four bergantinas he had sent to Buenos Aires in April and July turned up in Asunción. The effort to keep a Spanish settlement on the Río de la Plata had failed. Repeated assaults by Querandís, who shot arrows at settlers fishing in the river and set fire to Spanish houses, had left colonists wounded, demoralized, and near starvation. Winter flooding had canceled plans to move the colony to a safer location on the lower Paraná River. Then an earthquake at the end of October killed fourteen settlers.

Cabeza de Vaca must have welcomed his cousin and his many compatriots from Jerez. He had not seen them since he left Santa Catalina Island. But the loss of Buenos Aires was a setback.

A worse setback occurred in early February 1543. An Indian servant accidentally brushed a spark onto the thatch wall of a house in Asunción one night, kindling a fire that swept through the town and destroyed 80 percent of the homes during a four-day blaze. Settlers lost food, clothing, livestock, and shelter. Thousands of bushels of cornmeal and other supplies for the planned entrada went up in smoke.

Luckily, Irala returned soon after with good news. On January 6, he had reached an area about six hundred miles to the north—somewhere along the border of Brazil and Bolivia—that looked like a good base of operations for further exploration. He named it Puerto de los Reyes—"Port of the Kings"—in honor of the Christian holiday of Epiphany, or Kings' Day, celebrated on January 6 to mark the arrival of the three kings with gifts for the Christ child.

Various groups of people friendly to the Spaniards farmed the fertile region. The Spaniards called them Orejones (Big Ears) because they wore such large earplugs that their earlobes dangled on their shoulders. The most encouraging news was that Irala had met some captive Guaranís who knew about Alejo García's journey eighteen years earlier.

Cabeza de Vaca must have longed to depart right away,

but many urgent matters had to be dealt with first. Asunción had to be rebuilt, this time with more fire-resistant adobe. He muddied his own hands constructing a new church. He also gave needy settlers clothing and blankets from his own supplies and purchased food for them from the Indians.

During this difficult time, Venegas, Cáceres, and Cabrera—the three royal officials who had come with Mendoza—complained about not having enough say in the governance of the colony. To counter their complaints, Cabeza de Vaca offered to reimburse the taxes he no longer allowed them to collect, provided that Spanish courts agreed they had been deprived of rightful income. He then called a meeting to discuss government matters.

Aware that everyone wanted to find gold and silver, he steered the agenda toward the entrada and asked officials, captains, and clergy their views on how it should be organized. He received such a contradictory batch of opinions that he could safely do whatever he chose. He opted for speed. On June 8, he announced his plans to lead the entrada as soon as possible.

Two days later, several Guaraní headmen came to Cabeza de Vaca to report that two friars who had joined the expedition in Santa Catalina had left Asunción taking their daughters with them. When Cabeza de Vaca sent men to bring the friars and the thirty-five girls back, he discovered a conspiracy against his rule. The friars were walking to Santa Catalina in hopes of catching a ship to Europe. They carried with them letters from the royal officials accusing Cabeza de Vaca of misgovernment and requesting that Irala be made governor of the province. The friars seemed surprised that Cabeza de Vaca was still alive—the plan had been to assassinate him as soon as the friars departed.

Cabeza de Vaca arrested the officials and the notary who had prepared the letters and put them in jail. He decided not to punish Irala, assuming that he could win him over. Besides, he needed his help on the entrada. In the end, before leaving, he freed two of the royal officials, Dorantes and Cáceres, in order to have their services on the expedition as well. Perhaps he was being too lenient. But with many colonists malnourished or ill, he required all the able bodies he could muster. Besides, he believed that forgiveness made more allies than hard-nosed justice.

On September 8, ten bergantinas carrying four hundred Spaniards and 120 canoes with twelve hundred native allies formed a colorful procession up the river. At night they moored their boats and camped along the riverbank, their glittering campfires extending fully three miles, Pedro Hernández wrote later. They ate well, catching fish, otters, and capybaras, which the Spaniards called water-pigs.

Capybaras are the world's largest rodents. These tailless creatures, native to South America, can weigh as much as 140 pounds. They eat grass and water plants and are strong swimmers.

Hernández noticed that everyone looked "strong and lusty . . . as though they had just arrived from Spain."

Farther upriver, the flotilla split into two contingents so as not to overwhelm the people whose lands they were passing through. Cabeza de Vaca left wooden crosses to mark the winding route through various rivers and lagoons branching off from the Paraguay into the lands of the Orejones.

The second contingent had less luck. Suffocating in the tropical heat, several men took off their armor and helmets to tow a bergantina. Indians attacked and killed five of the men. Word went out among the various native groups that the invaders had soft heads. The attackers began recruiting allies to help rid the land of Spaniards.

Cabeza de Vaca took formal possession of Puerto de los Reyes and through interpreters explained the requerimiento to the Indians. He set men to work building a fort and a church and issued rules to prevent his men and his Indian allies from infringing on the rights of the Orejones. He also sent two Spaniards farther north to other groups who traded in gold and silver and might be willing to furnish a guide to their sources.

The men returned with a Guaraní who had remained among the gold-trading Indians after taking part in a raid for precious metals many years earlier. Cabeza de Vaca seized the opportunity. Leaving one hundred Spaniards and twice as many Guaranís to guard the bergantinas, Cabeza de Vaca marched out of Puerto de los Reyes. He led three hundred Spaniards and hundreds of Indian allies, many of them women carrying the fifty-pound allotment of manioc flour for each expedition member. It was late November, and the summer rainy season was just beginning. The air crawled with insects. At night vampire bats bit uncovered ears and toes.

Five days later, the guide admitted he was lost. Other Guaranís in the area offered help from relatives who lived two days' journey away. Men sent to scout the possibility brought back discouraging news. For two days each way, they had hacked through underbrush so dense that much of the time they crawled on hands and knees. The nearest settled area, where the "Lords of the Metal" lived, they said, was a sixteen-day trek beyond, through more wilderness where warlike hunters sometimes roamed.

Captains on the expedition advised returning to Puerto de los Reyes because provisions were low. The men had not rationed their flour but ate as much as they pleased. The noise of hundreds of people crashing through the forest, moreover, had scared off game they might have hunted for food.

Cabeza de Vaca reluctantly agreed. But he sent one of his captains, Francisco de Ribera, with a small party to learn the route and find out more about the Lords of the Metal so that he could plan another entrada.

Cabeza de Vaca remained optimistic, but during the next four months, the odds mounted against success. With more than two thousand extra mouths to feed, the Orejones's food supplies were dwindling. In mid-December, Cabeza de Vaca sent two parties out to purchase provisions from Indians farther north. One of the captains brought back plenty of cornmeal, but his efforts to barter peacefully had met with hostility. He had killed two Indians in self-defense, he reported, and when the rest fled, he took food but left plenty for their own needs.

The Indians who had earlier attacked the expedition, meanwhile, were inciting the peaceable Orejones to rebel against the Spaniards. It was not just the Spanish they objected to but also the Guaranís, who, contrary to Cabeza de Vaca's rules, were taking local Indians as slaves.

In January 1544, Francisco de Ribera and his men returned, all wounded by Indian arrows. He had reached a village of the Lords of the Metal after a strenuous 210-mile hike through the wilderness. He saw many signs of their wealth—quantities of cotton cloth, corn, and silver platters, hatchets, and bracelets—but the Indians attacked the Spaniards without warning. Cabeza de Vaca began making plans to go there, but it was impossible to start right away because rains had caused extensive flooding.

The abundant rain also brought illness. The Spaniards attributed the disease to the bad-smelling water, for its stink, they thought, contaminated the air. More likely, it was the mosquitoes breeding in pools of standing water that caused the fever, chills, and the recurring bouts of illness—typical symptoms of malaria—that Cabeza de Vaca and Pedro Hernández describe in their accounts.

The other captain Cabeza de Vaca sent for provisions returned at the end of January with no food. Instead, he brought stories he heard from the Native Americans. One tale told of a tribe of fierce women warriors and another of a black, eagle-faced people who were so wealthy that they made all their tools of gold and silver. Cabeza de Vaca, however, at that point was too ill even to hear his official report. Almost everyone in hot, sticky Puerto de los Reyes had fallen sick. One Spaniard and several Guaranís died.

Seeing the invaders' weakness, the Orejones grew bolder in their resistance. They captured small parties of men out fishing and killed them. They attacked the fort, and in one battle, fifty-eight Spaniards lost their lives. In February, Cabeza de Vaca was well enough to consult with his officers and declare war on the Orejones, his hopes for a peaceful conquest dashed against the hard fact of Native American opposition.

By the time the waters began to dry up in March, food supplies were once again low. The comptroller Cáceres presented a strongly worded demand to evacuate Puerto de los Reyes and return to Asunción. Cabeza de Vaca listened to arguments on both sides, but in the end, he knew the health of his people and his Guaraní allies was at stake.

As everyone prepared to leave, Cabeza de Vaca told his men to return to their families all the women, many of them daughters of local headmen, who had become their servants and mistresses during their five-month stay in Puerto de los Reyes. The king ordered, he reminded them, that no Indians be removed from their lands. Irala and some of the other Spanish captains, who considered the women their personal property, were furious. The Orejones, on the other hand, were pleased. Cabeza de Vaca called together their chiefs and gave them presents, telling them that he hoped to return soon. "Thus I left them in total peace and concord."

CONQUISTADOR
IN CHAINS

Spears and arrows flew at the flotilla as it sailed downstream toward Asunción. The bergantinas stuck close together, with the more vulnerable Guaraní canoes tucked safely in the middle. Most of the men, Cabeza de Vaca included, were "very weak and sick, on the point of death." Those well enough to man the guns shot at the war-painted combatants lining the riverbank.

During the perilous twelve-day journey, resentment against Cabeza de Vaca simmered. The great entrada had yielded no riches to boast of in letters home and to pay off years of accumulated debt. No captured enemies came as slaves to plant and harvest crops. Cabeza de Vaca had even deprived the expedition members of the women friendly headmen had provided, women who might have consoled wounded bodies and pride. "It really would have been no great loss had he died at this time," the German Schmidel commented, "for he really commanded no great respect among us."

Irala, a few other disgruntled captains, and the royal officials saw opportunity in this anger. Ever since Cabeza de Vaca had arrived in Asunción, these leaders had been angling to rid themselves of this governor who had taken away their tax revenues, their female servants and mistresses, and their slaves. Before leaving Puerto de los Reyes, Cáceres had made sure that no garrison remained there. Having the entire colony in one place would make it easier to stage a coup.

The plotters began to recruit support as soon as they arrived. Taking aside men who had remained in Asunción, Irala told them that Cabeza de Vaca intended to confiscate their property, homes, and Indian women to give to those who went on the expedition. The officials were going to challenge Cabeza de Vaca on this issue, he said, and feared that they would be arrested. Irala asked them to arm themselves in secret and be ready to defend the royal officials.

On the night of April 25, 1544, the four royal officials and an armed escort burst into Cabeza de Vaca's bedroom. Shouting "Liberty! Liberty! Long live the king!" they pointed daggers, swords, and loaded harquebuses and crossbows at the fever-dazed man. Hauling the governor out of bed, the men dragged Cabeza de Vaca into the streets and wakened the town with their cries.

One hundred men recruited to defend the royal officials rushed out, swords drawn. Cries of "Down with the tyrant!" filled the night air as the men spread Irala's lies about Cabeza de Vaca. Some, however, seeing that it was the royal officials who were arresting the governor, not the other way around, realized that they had been duped. They tried to stop the arrest, but the officials hustled the governor into the house of the royal treasurer, Garci Venegas, and ordered everyone off the streets.

The officials shackled Cabeza de Vaca in a small storage room and set men they trusted to guard his door twenty-four hours a day. In the weeks that followed, they surrounded the house and several others with a stout stockade, set deep into the ground to foil any attempt to tunnel under it. They turned nearby homes into barracks housing fifty men-at-arms who supported the conspiracy.

The royal officials appointed Irala to govern the colony and imposed strict laws. To prevent efforts to rescue Cabeza de Vaca, they set a curfew and forbid public meetings—even of two people speaking in the street. Fearing that Cabeza de Vaca's supporters might try to escape to Spain to denounce their actions, they scuttled all boats.

Irala jailed Cabeza de Vaca's cousin Pedro Estopiñan, his nephew Alonso Riquelme de Guzmán, and other friends and relatives from Jerez, priests who preached against the mutineers, and anyone else who acted or spoke in his favor. When these actions did not stop resistance to Irala's rule, he threatened to behead Cabeza de Vaca the minute anyone tried to rescue him. Cabeza de Vaca was asked to write a statement telling his supporters to abandon all efforts to free him. Better to go to Spain under arrest, Cabeza de Vaca wrote, than "that on my behalf a single drop of blood should be shed."

Meanwhile, the rebels looted Cabeza de Vaca's belongings and used them to reward supporters. They rifled through legal documents Cabeza de Vaca had gathered to send to the king and inked out mentions of their own misdeeds. To gain popularity with men who had chafed under Cabeza de Vaca's regulations, they reversed his policies toward their Guaraní allies, allowing settlers to force Indians to work without pay and to buy and sell Indian women. To appease the Guaranís, they rescinded the law against eating human flesh.

That summer, to gain legal control of the colony, the rebels began to prepare a case against Cabeza de Vaca's governorship to present to the court in Spain. They knew what kind of charges most hurt conquistadors in the eyes of the king: abuse of Native Americans, disobedience of royal orders, and setting their own authority above that of the king.

Finding no examples of mistreatment, the conspirators seized on the few instances when Cabeza de Vaca had resorted to warfare and exaggerated the casualties. A captain who had killed two Indians in self-defense when he tried to buy food was accused of committing a massacre. They further claimed that the captain stole all the Indians' food, leaving thousands of innocent people to starve to death.

As annoying to the rebels as Cabeza de Vaca's kindness to Native Americans was what they considered his arrogance. They looked for ways to show that he usurped royal power. He had flown a banner with the Cabeza de Vaca coat of arms from the mast of a bergantina during the entrada. The rebels claimed that removing the royal banner used on earlier expeditions was proof that he put his own authority above that of the king.

A number of witnesses recalled occasions when the governor had angrily shouted the equivalent of "I'm the boss here!" at them. They omitted mentioning whatever provoked the outburst, which was probably their saying that Irala had permitted something that Cabeza de Vaca had just told them not to do—such as beat their servants. Witnesses who dared to deny that Cabeza de Vaca was putting himself above the king were told, "They are not asking you that."

For close to a year, terror reigned in Asunción. The conspirators sent patrols into the streets at night, put sentries on rooftops to keep an eye on all activity, and planted spies to report on suspicious comments. Some witnesses were tortured into testifying against Cabeza de Vaca and tortured again if they recanted. Stubborn defenders of Cabeza de Vaca were left crippled for life. Brawling between opponents and defenders of the jailed governor led to beatings, stabbings, and drownings. Even the clergy became embroiled in fights.

Cabeza de Vaca's supporters meanwhile met secretly to prepare their own testimony about what was going on in the colony, which Cabeza de Vaca's notary Pedro Hernández took down in correct legal form. Friends kept Cabeza de Vaca aware of what they were doing for him with the help of a Guaraní woman who brought him his food. The guards strip-searched the woman but never found the papers rolled tightly, encased in wax, and skillfully tied under her toes with cotton thread. One of the papers smuggled in and out was a document for him to sign declaring Captain Juan de Salazar his successor.

Among Cabeza de Vaca's loyal supporters were some carpenters working on a small caravel being built to send him to Spain for trial. These men hollowed out a beam to create a space in which to hide letters defending his governorship.

On March 7, 1545, shortly before midnight, the royal officials came with an armed escort to Cabeza de Vaca's tiny cell. Lifting the ailing prisoner, chains and all, from his bed, they carried him out into the night. Seeing the stars for the first time in almost a year, Cabeza de Vaca begged permission to pray. Kneeling on the ground, he thanked God he was still alive.

As the conspirators hustled him down to the river, Cabeza de Vaca managed to shout that he was appointing Captain

Juan de Salazar as deputy governor. The treasurer Venegas threatened him with a dagger, but Cabeza de Vaca repeated his cry three times. He hoped that even after his departure, his faithful friends would overthrow Irala.

The hastily-built caravel slipped down the dark river with Cabeza de Vaca chained inside. Among the twenty-five men crowded aboard were two of the royal officials, Venegas and Cabrera, who went with him to present their accusations at the Spanish court. Men-at-arms guarded the prisoner.

A week later in Asunción, Captain Juan de Salazar presented Irala with the document declaring that Cabeza de Vaca had appointed him deputy governor. About 120 settlers made a show of support for Salazar, but Irala quickly put the uprising down. He arrested Salazar and the notary Pedro Hernández and sent them by boat to catch up with the ship bound for Europe. At an island in the Río de la Plata estuary where the ship took on the additional prisoners, the shipwright who had hidden the documents got word to Cabeza de Vaca about where they were.

Cabeza de Vaca faced more than the usual perils on the voyage to Europe. First, his food made him ill. When he found it contained chickpea-sized lumps of realgar—a reddishorange mineral that contains the poison arsenic sulfide—he refused to eat. After four days, too hungry to hold out any longer, he used a remedy he had brought with him from Spain—olive oil with a piece of unicorn horn (probably narwhal horn) in it to give it special medicinal virtues. Either it helped or the poisoning stopped, for Cabeza de Vaca recovered.

Then a terrible storm battered the small ship for several days. Wracked with guilt, Venegas and Cabrera filed the shackles off Cabeza de Vaca's legs and begged his forgiveness.

When the storm abated, they promised to throw all the letters accusing him overboard if he would withdraw his complaints against them. Not devious enough himself to pretend to agree, Cabeza de Vaca refused. Being unshackled, however, apparently gave him enough freedom of movement on the ship to remove his supporters' letters from their hiding place so that he would have them safely on his person when he disembarked. He was confident the letters would prove his innocence.

The flimsy ship held together in the storm, but salt water rushing into the hold spoiled much of the food. Unwilling to stop at Santa Catalina or Hispaniola for provisions out of fear their prisoner would escape, the two officials pressed on. When they reached the Azores, everyone was half starved.

In the Azores, Cabeza de Vaca and his friends managed to take passage on a different ship. It meant that Venegas and Cabrera arrived in Spain first, but it gained them no real advantage. The Council of the Indies accepted accusatory documents from both sides and freed everyone on bail.

Cabeza de Vaca went home to Jerez to write his official report, the *Relación general*, for the king. Never intended for wider publication, this account offers a glimpse into Cabeza de Vaca's state of mind that fall of 1545. He seems bewildered by the malice of Irala and the royal officials. One biographer suggests that he saw himself as being tested by God.

In the *Relación general,* Cabeza de Vaca points out how carefully he observed all the stipulations of his contract. He always consulted with royal officials, officers, and clergy, and he listened to their advice. He followed the letter and the spirit of the king's laws in his dealings with friendly and hostile natives. If anything, he sounds to the modern reader a little self-righteous and in places a bit whiny. But the report also sounds very honest and to the point. He does not rant about the immorality and lawlessness in Asunción when he arrived, but the report shows how he worked to correct it. Like the *Relación* of the Narváez expedition, it is the story of an intelligent, level-headed leader who remains optimistic and never panics, even in the direst circumstances.

In this account, we see for the first time his firmness with resistance from native peoples and his efforts to balance the needs of his own men with those of Native Americans. As in the *Relación*, it is clear he preferred settled Indians, who saw the advantages of alliance with European civilization, and sympathized less with warlike hunters and gatherers, who fought European incursion into their lands. But even so, he tried to be scrupulously fair to them.

By early December, the *Relación general* was complete. Cabeza de Vaca sent it to the king and prayed for the best outcome. The Council of the Indies nevertheless decided to put Cabeza de Vaca on trial. That winter the judge appointed to the case drew up a list of thirty-four charges against him. Every grievance the royal officials had gathered was on it.

From what historians know from other sources, whether friendly to Cabeza de Vaca, neutral, or in opposition to his governorship, most of the charges were outright lies or twisted variations on the truth. In fact, the accusations painted a portrait of such an evil and dangerous man that the Council of the Indies ordered his imprisonment. In February 1546, Cabeza de Vaca was once again in jail, this time in Madrid.

ꞅeveꞑꞇeeꞑ

TRIAL AND
VINDICATION

Cabeza de Vaca repeatedly petitioned for release from jail. In April, after posting a bond of two thousand ducats, he was put on house arrest at the home of a courtier. By September he gained the freedom of the court—that is, he had to remain with the royal court as it traveled around Spain. The following September, he was given "the kingdom as his prison." He was free to go wherever he wished within Spain so long as, if summoned, he reported to court within thirty days.

By early summer 1546, Cabeza de Vaca was busy collecting testimony from friends, relations, and people who had known him at the Duke of Medina Sidonia's court, on the Italian campaign, and during his military service in Spain. Almost everything known about Cabeza de Vaca's life before the Narváez expedition to Florida comes from answers these people gave to questions drawn up by Cabeza de Vaca and his lawyer. Each witness testified in closed session in front of two notaries—one representing Cabeza de Vaca and one assigned by the court. Gathering testimony took time, for the witnesses were scattered over more than twenty Spanish towns.

During the next five years, five different attorneys prosecuted Cabeza de Vaca's case. On March 18, 1551, six councilors of the Indies found Cabeza de Vaca guilty. They stripped him of his titles, banned him for life from returning to America, and ordered him to spend five years military service—supplying his own horse and weapons—in Oran, a Spanish colony in northern Africa.

Cabeza de Vaca immediately appealed his sentence and began gathering more testimonies. In August 1552, the judges ruled he did not have to serve in northern Africa and reduced his banishment from the Indies to only Río de la Plata.

It took eight years, but at last, Cabeza de Vaca was "free and discharged from obligation." He remained at court to seek reimbursement for everything the conspirators stole from him in Río de la Plata. Meanwhile, relatives from Jerez had begun asking him to represent them at the royal court. Soon the city council of Jerez was paying him to work on its behalf as well. Cabeza de Vaca had restored his good reputation.

To further banish the shadow of his enemies' accusations, Cabeza de Vaca requested permission to publish a new edition of the *Relación* together with an account of his years in Río de la Plata written by his loyal supporter, Pedro Hernández. In 1555 the book was published in Valladolid. With a new title, *Naufragios*—literally, "Shipwrecks," but also translatable as "Calamities" or "Woes"—and divided into chapters, the *Relación* was revised to appeal to a wider audience. Pedro Hernández's account, also divided into chapters, was entitled *Comentarios* (Commentaries), evoking classical histories of ancient Roman warriors. Together the two chronicles portray Cabeza de Vaca's struggle to bring about a humane conquest in both North and South America.

Publishing the book was Cabeza de Vaca's ultimate victory over his enemies. Its popularity assured that his name would go down in history as the conquistador who defended the Indians of the Americas.

Few documents survive concerning Cabeza de Vaca's last years. In 1555 he lived in Seville, where he must have heard constant news of the New World as ships came and went. Apparently, Maria Marmolejo had looked after his property well—as many conquistadors' wives did during the long years their husbands were away. For, in spite of all his losses on his two expeditions to the Indies, in 1559 he had the funds to ransom a nephew captured in northern Africa.

At some point, Cabeza de Vaca returned to his hometown. He probably died there and was buried in the family vault with his famous grandfather. Neither the date nor the cause of death is known. He left no children, only his book, to carry on his name.

In the later 1500s, explorers, missionaries, historians, geographers, and political theorists all consulted Cabeza de Vaca's writings for information and inspiration. Already in 1556, Gian Battista Ramusio, a well-known collector of accounts of pioneering voyages (among them Marco Polo's), had translated the *Relación* into Italian. In the early 1600s, English versions were first published. Today many editions and translations of the *Relación*, biographies, novels based on Cabeza de Vaca's life, scholarly articles and books, and at least one film about him are available in both Spanish and English.

To many Americans in both North and South America, Cabeza de Vaca is a hero, admired for being a defender of Native Americans, as well as an extraordinary man who crossed two continents barefoot.

Michael J. Waters, a modern artist, created this watercolor showing Estevanico (Dorantes's African slave) and two Native Americans on an expedition in Mexico led by the friar Marcos de Niza in 1539.

WHAT HAPPENED
TO THE OTHERS

Andrés Dorantes, who traveled across Texas and
Mexico with Cabeza de Vaca, intended to return to Spain with
him in the spring of 1537, but Dorantes was on one of the
leaky ships that never made it to Havana. He gave up and
returned to Mexico City and his new wife, the rich widow of
a conquistador. His son Baltasar wrote a chronicle about New
Spain, in which he mentioned the "miracles and marvels" of
his father's odyssey with Cabeza de Vaca.

Alonso del Castillo, another of the four survivors of the
Narváez expedition who crossed the North American continent, also remained in New Spain and married another rich
widow. The Spanish viceroy played matchmaker for both
men. Both Dorantes and Castillo served the viceroy in various administrative posts, rising to positions of importance in
the colonial government.

Estevanico, Dorantes's African slave, was the only one of the survivors to return to the lands they traversed. The Spanish viceroy, eager to start his own explorations to the north, purchased Estevanico from Dorantes to serve as a guide. In March 1539, he sent Estevanico on an expedition led by the friar Marcos de Niza. A month later, somewhere in northern Sonora, local Indians assaulted Estevanico and a scouting party of Native American allies. A few of the allies escaped to tell of Estevanico's death in the attack.

Two accounts of the expedition of Hernando de Soto more than ten years after the Narváez expedition give conflicting news of Doroteo Teodoro and the African, who were left behind during the boat trip across the Gulf of Mexico. One account says that de Soto's men found them living in a village inland from the coast. The other reports that they were killed by Indians.

Another report tells of the demise of Diego de Alcaraz, the leader of the slave hunters who were the first Spaniards Cabeza de Vaca met after crossing North America. Alcaraz was killed in a massacre when Indians revolted against him at a Spanish outpost in Sonora in the 1540s.

Domingo Martínez de Irala continued his reign of terror in Asunción. Even his admirer Schmidel admitted the violence. For two years after Cabeza de Vaca left, he wrote, "no man was safe from the other." In 1547 Irala led an expedition across the Gran Chaco wilderness of central South America and discovered that the gold and silver mines he sought had already been found by Spaniards from Peru. He later expanded Spanish control over the land Cabeza de Vaca had claimed on his walk from the Atlantic coast to Asunción. At last, in 1555, the Spanish king officially named Irala governor of the colony (an earlier replacement having died en route). Irala died of appendicitis the next year.

The royal treasurer of the Río de la Plata colony, Felipe de Cáceres, remained in Asunción. In the 1560s, he secured an appointment as lieutenant governor of Río de la Plata while a newly appointed governor traveled to Spain. He soon made himself a hated dictator, and for two years, he held sway over an increasingly rebellious colony. Arrested in an uprising in 1572, he was jailed for a year and sent to Spain for trial. On the way to Spain, he escaped. He died some time after that, a fugitive from justice.

Alonso Cabrera and Garci Venegas, the two royal officials who returned to Spain with Cabeza de Vaca, soon came to grief. Cabrera went mad and killed his wife (Pedro Hernández reported) and ended his days in a lunatic asylum, while Venegas "died a sudden, terrible death, his eyes having fallen out of his head."

Bartolomé de las Casas continued his struggle against the cruel and abusive treatment of Native Americans, using Cabeza de Vaca's accounts to buttress his arguments that Indians were good, reasonable people open to Christian education. He trained missionaries for the New World and wrote numerous books and tracts advocating a more humane conquest and rule in the Americas. He died in 1566.

New World wealth made Spain the greatest European power of the age and a major center of European culture well into the 1600s. Spanish colonial rule lasted in Latin America for almost three hundred years until the early 1800s. In that century, Spanish descendants, Native Americans, and people of mixed race joined together to overthrow Spanish rule, abolish slavery, and establish independent nations.

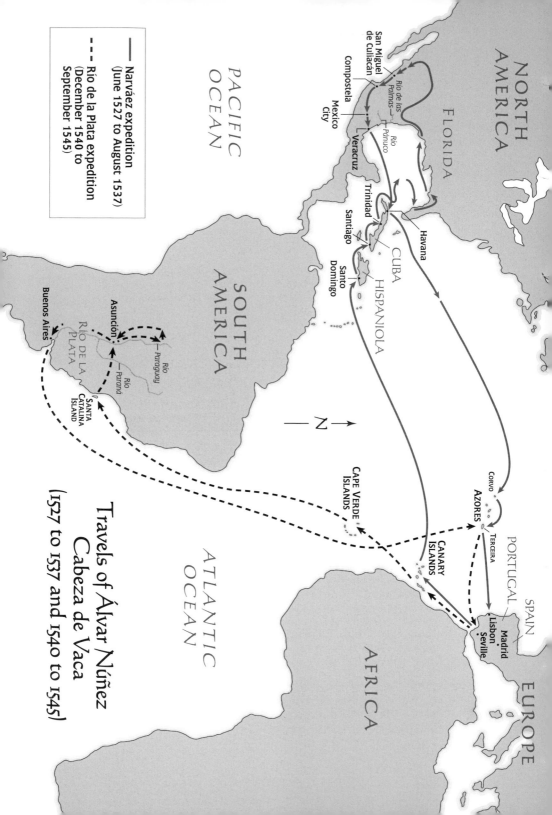

NORTH AMERICA

PACIFIC OCEAN

FLORIDA

San Miguel de Culiacán
Compostela
Río de las Palmas
Mexico City
Río Pánuco
Veracruz
Trinidad
Santiago
Santo Domingo
Havana
CUBA
HISPANIOLA

SOUTH AMERICA

Buenos Aires
Asunción
RÍO DE LA PLATA
Río Paraguay
Río Paraná
SANTA CATALINA ISLAND

N →

CAPE VERDE ISLANDS

ATLANTIC OCEAN

AZORES
CORVO
TERCEIRA
CANARY ISLANDS

PORTUGAL
SPAIN
Madrid
Lisbon
Seville

AFRICA

EUROPE

— Narváez expedition
(June 1527 to August 1537)

- - - Río de la Plata expedition
(December 1540 to September 1545)

Travels of Álvar Núñez
Cabeza de Vaca
(1527 to 1537 and 1540 to 1545)

Source Notes

7 Álvar Núñez Cabeza de Vaca, *Chronicle of the Narváez Expedition*, trans. Fanny Bandelier and rev. Harold Augenbraum (New York: Penguin Books, 2002), 32.

10 Diego de Valera, *Crónica de los reyes católicos*, ed. Juan de M. Carriazo (Madrid: Molina, 1927), 108.

12 "Testimony of Rodrigo León," Justicia 1131 8A, General Archive of the Indies (Seville, SPN), in Morris Bishop, *The Odyssey of Cabeza de Vaca* (New York: Century Co., 1933), 9.

14 Hipólito Sancho de Sopranis, "Notas y documentos sobre Álvar Núñez Cabeza de Vaca," *Revista de Indias* 23, no. 91–92 (1963), 238.

16 Bernal Diaz del Castillo, *The Conquest of New Spain* (London: Penguin Books, 1963), 9.

19 José Ignacio Mantecón, ed., *Información de méritos y servicios de Alonso García Bravo* (Mexico City: Imprenta Universitaria de la UNAM, 1956), 39, in Rolena Adorno and Patrick Charles Pautz, eds., *Álvar Núñez Cabeza de Vaca: His Account, His Life, and the Expedition of Pánfile de Narváez* (Lincoln: University of Nebraska Press, 1999), 3:257.

19 Gonzalo Fernández de Oviedo y Valdés, *Historia general y natural de las Indias* (Madrid: Ediciones Atlas, 1992), 4:59.

19 Oviedo y Valdés, *Historia general,* 4:285.

20 "Capitulations between Charles V and Pánfilo de Narváez," in *New American World: A Documentary History of North America to 1612*, David B. Quinn, ed. (New York: Arno Press, 1979) 2:4.

22 Jon Cowans, ed. *Early Modern Spain: A Documentary History* (Philadelphia: University of Pennsylvania Press, 2003), 34.

23 Ibid., 35–36.

23 Quinn, *New American World* 2:4.

24 Ibid., 6.

24 "Instructions Given to Cabeza de Vaca for his Observance as Treasurer to the King of Spain," in Buckingham Smith, trans., *Relation of Cabeza de Vaca* (New York, 1871; repr., Ann Arbor, MI: University Microfilms, 1966), 221.

26 The map is reproduced in Adorno and Pautz, 2: 36

27 Pietro Martire d'Anghiera, *Décadas del Nuevo Mundo* (Santo Domingo: Sociedad Dominicana de Bibliófilos, 1989), 443, in Adorno and Pautz, *Cabeza de Vaca*, 3:241.

27 Oviedo y Valdés, *Historia general,* 4:321.

28 Diego García de Palacio, *Instrucción nautical para navegar* (Madrid, 1944), fol. 2, in Pablo Pérez-Mallaína, *Spain's Men of the Sea: Daily Life on the Indies Fleets in the Sixteenth Century* (Baltimore: Johns Hopkins Press, 1998), 23.

30 Álvar Núñez Cabeza de Vaca, *Chronicle of the Narváez Expedition*, trans. Fanny Bandelier and rev. Harold Augenbraum (New York: Penguin Books, 2002), 5.

31 Ibid., 6–7.

36 Ibid., 10–11.

37 Ibid., 11.

37 Ibid.

38 Ibid., 12.
38 Ibid., 13.
46 Ibid., 20.
47 Ibid., 23.
48 Ibid., 24.
49 Ibid., 26.
51 Ibid., 27.
52 Ibid., 29.
52 Ibid., 30.
53 Ibid., 38.
54–55 Ibid., 33.
55 Ibid.
55 Ibid., 33–34.
58 Ibid., 40.
58 Ibid.
62 Ibid., 44.
63 Ibid., 45.
64 Basil C. Hedrick and Carroll L. Riley, eds., *The Journey of the Vaca Party: The Account of the Narváez Expedition, 1528–1536, as Related by Gonzalo Fernández de Oviedo y Valdés*, (Carbondale: University Museum, Southern Illinois University, 1974), 33–35.
66 Cabeza de Vaca, *Chronicle*, 50.
67 Ibid., 53–54.
69 Ibid., 57–58.
69 Ibid., 58.
70 Ibid., 61.
71 Ibid., 62.
72 Hedrick and Riley, *The Journey of the Vaca Party*, 47.
72 Cabeza de Vaca, *Chronicle*, 63.
72 Ibid.
72 Hedrick and Riley, *The Journey of the Vaca Party*, 47.
72 Ibid., 48.
74 Cabeza de Vaca, *Chronicle*, 67.
74 Ibid., 73.
75 Ibid., 76.
77 Ibid., 78.
77 Ibid., 79.
78 Ibid., 81.
78 Ibid.
81 Ibid., 85.
82 Ibid., 86.
83 Ibid.
84 Ibid., 88.
86 Ibid., 90.
87 Ibid.
87 Ibid.
88 Ibid., 93
90 Ibid., 96.
91 Hedrick and Riley, *Journey of the Vaca Party*, 67.
93 Cabeza de Vaca, *Chronicle*, 98.
93 Ibid., 99.
93 Ibid., 101.
95 Patronato 57, no. 4 General Archive of the Indies (Seville, Spain), ramo 1, f11r, in Adorno and Pautz, *Cabeza de Vaca*, 2:392.
103 Ysabel de Guevara, "Hardships in the Río de la Plata Region," in Cowans, *Early Modern Spain: A Documentary History*, 83.
104 Lawrence A. Clayton, Vernon James Knight Jr., and Edward C. Moore, eds., *The De Soto Chronicles* (Tuscaloosa: University of Alabama Press, 1993), 1:48.
106 Pope Paul III, "*Sublimus Dei*," 1537, *Papal Encyclicals Online*, May 29, 1537 http://www.papalencyclicals.net/Paul03/p3subli.htm (February 17, 2006).
111 "The Commentaries of Álvar Núñez Cabeza de Vaca," in Luis L. Domínguez, ed., *The Conquest of the River Plate 1535–1555* (London: Hakluyt Society, 1891; repr., New York: Burt Franklin, 1964), 99.
114 *Relación general,* in Manuel Serrano y Sanz, ed., *Relación de los naufragios y commentarios* (Madrid: Victoriano Suárez, 1906), 2:8.
115 "Commentaries," in Dominguez, *The Conquest of the River Plate 1535–1555,* 110.
115 Ibid., 111.
115 Ibid., 107.
116 Ibid., 112.

118 Ibid., 124.
118 Serrano y Sanz, *Relación general*, 15.
122 "The Voyage of Ulrich Schmidt," in Dominguez, *The Conquest of the River Plate 1535–1555*, 41.
123 "Commentaries," in Dominguez, *The Conquest of the River Plate 1535–1555*, 132.
123 Ibid., 137.
124 Ibid., 153.
125 Ibid., 155.
125 Ibid.
131 "Commentaries," in Domínguez, *The Conquest of the River Plate 1535–1555*, 185
134 Serrano y Sanz, *Relación general*, 58.
135 Ibid., 58–59.
135–136 "Voyage of Ulrich Schmidt" in Domínguez, *The Conquest of the River Plate 1535–1555*, 50.
137 Serrano y Sanz, *Relación general*, 65–66.

138 Pedro Hernández, "Relación," in Serrano y Sanz, *Relacción general*, 2:346.
143 Justicia 1131, General Archive of the Indies (Seville, SPN), in Adorno and Pautz, *Cabeza de Vaca*, 1:395.
144 "Comentarios," in Serrano y Sanz, *Relacción general*, 1:367, as translated by Adorno and Pautz, *Cabeza de Vaca*, 1:401.
147 Baltasar Dorantes de Carranza, *Sumaria relación de las cosas de la Nueva España* (Mexico City: Editorial Porrúa, 1987), 229.
148 "Voyage of Ulrich Schmidt," in Domínguez, *The Conquest of the River Plate 1535–1555*, 54.
149 "Commentaries," in Domínguez, *The Conquest of the River Plate 1535–1555*, 262.

Bibliography

Adorno, Rolena, and Patrick Charles Pautz, eds. *Álvar Núñez Cabeza de Vaca: His Account, His Life, and the Expedition of Pánfilo de Narváez.* 3 vols. Lincoln: University of Nebraska Press, 1999.

Bishop, Morris. *The Odyssey of Cabeza de Vaca.* New York: Century Co, 1933.

Cabeza de Vaca, Álvar Núñez. *Chronicle of the Narváez Expedition.* Translated by Fanny Bandelier. Revised by Harold Augenbraum. New York: Penguin Books, 2002.

Cowans, Jon, ed. *Early Modern Spain: A Documentary History.* Philadelphia: University of Pennsylvania Press, 2003. A selection of Spanish historical documents translated into English.

Domínguez, Luis L. *The Conquest of the River Plate 1535–1555.* London: Hakluyt Society, 1891. Reprint, New York: Burt Franklin, 1964.

Hanke, Lewis. *The Spanish Struggle for Justice in the Conquest of America.* Boston: Little, Brown and Co., 1965.

Hedrick, Basil C., and Carroll L. Riley, eds. *The Journey of the Vaca Party: The Account of the Narváez Expedition, 1528–1536, as Related by Gonzalo Fernández de Oviedo y Valdes*. Carbondale: University Museum, Southern Illinois University, 1974.

Hoffman, Paul E. "Narváez and Cabeza de Vaca in Florida," in *The Forgotten Centuries: Indians and Europeans in the American South, 1521–1704*, 50–69. Edited by Charles Hudson and Carmen Chaves Tesser. Athens: University of Georgia Press, 1994.

Howard, David A. *Conquistador in Chains: Cabeza de Vaca and the Indians of the Americas*. Tuscaloosa: University of Alabama Press, 1997.

Krieger, Alex D. *We Came Naked and Barefoot: The Journey of Cabeza de Vaca Across North America*. Edited by Margery H. Krieger. Austin: University of Texas Press, 2002.

Lopez, Adalberto. "A Tradition of Autonomy." Chap. 1 in *The Revolt of The Comuneros, 1721–1735, A Study in the Colonial History of Paraguay*. Cambridge, MA: Schenkman Publishing Co, 1976.

Morison, Samuel Eliot. "The Conquest of the River Plate, 1534–1580" in *The European Discovery of America, the Southern Voyages A.D. 1492–1616* (New York: Oxford University Press, 1974), 562–584.

Oviedo y Valdés, Gonzalo Fernández de. *Historia general y natural de las Indias*. 5 vols. Madrid: Ediciones Atlas, 1992.

Parry, John H., and Robert G. Keith, eds. *New Iberian World*. 5 vols. New York: Times Books, 1984.

Pérez-Mallaína, Pablo. *Spain's Men of the Sea: Daily Life on the Indies Fleets in the Sixteenth Century*. Baltimore: Johns Hopkins Press, 1998.

Phillips, William D., Jr., and Carla Rahn Phillips. *The Worlds of Christopher Columbus*. Cambridge: Cambridge University Press, 1992.

Pike, Ruth. *Aristocrats and Traders: Sevillian Society in the Sixteenth Century*. Ithaca, NY: Cornell University Press, 1972.

Quinn, David B., ed. *New American World: A Documentary History of North America to 1612*. 5 vols. New York: Arno Press, 1979.

Restall, Matthew. *Seven Myths of the Spanish Conquest*. New York: Oxford University Press, 2003.

Schneider, Paul. *Brutal Journey: The Epic Story of the First Crossing of North America*. New York: Henry Holt and Company, 2006.

Serrano y Sanz, Manuel, ed. *Relación de los naufragios y Comentarios de Álvar Núñez Cabeza de Vaca*. 2 vols. Madrid: Victoriano Suárez, 1906.

Steward, Julian H., ed. *Handbook of South American Indians*. 7 vols. New York: Cooper Square Publishers, 1963.

Wood, Michael. *Conquistadors*. Berkeley: University of California Press, 2000.

Further Reading and Websites

Books

Argentina in Pictures. Minneapolis: Twenty-first Century Books, 1994.

Burgan, Michael. *The Spanish Conquest of America*. New York: Chelsea House, 2006.

Johnston, Lissa. *Crossing a Continent: The Incredible Journey of Cabeza de Vaca*. Austin, TX: Eakins Press, 2005.

Maestro, Betsy, and Giulio Maestro. *Exploration and Conquest: The Americas after Columbus, 1500–1620*. New York: Lothrop, Lee and Shepard, 1994.

Marrin, Albert. *Empires Lost and Won: The Spanish Heritage in the Southwest*. New York: Atheneum, 1997.

Mattox, Jake, ed. *Explorers of the New World*. Farmington Hills, MI: Greenhaven Press, 2004.

Mexico in Pictures. Minneapolis: Twenty-first Century Books, 1996.

Shepherd, Elizabeth. *The Discoveries of Esteban the Black*. New York: Dodd, Mead, and Co., 1970.

Spain in Pictures. Minneapolis: Twenty-first Century Books, 1997.

Wojciechowska, Maia. *Odyssey of Courage: The Story of Álvar Núñez Cabeza de Vaca*. New York: Atheneum, 1965. Reprint, New York: Scribner's, 2000.

Wulffson, Don. *Before Columbus: Early Voyages to the Americas*. Minneapolis: Twenty-First Century Books, 2008.

Websites

Cabeza de Vaca in North America
http://www.floridahistory.com/cabeza.html
Donald E. Sheppard argues that Cabeza de Vaca took a more northern route across the continent. The website shows many photographs along the proposed route across central Texas, New Mexico, and Arizona. It also includes information about navigation and translations of relevant documents.

Cabeza de Vaca Relación Digitization and Access Project
http://www.library.txstate.edu/swwc/cdv/
This site ditigally reproduces the 1555 edition of the *Relación* with an accompanying translation about Cabeza de Vaca and Native Americans and analyzes key scenes in Nicolas Echevarria's 1991 film *Cabeza de Vaca*. The bibliography lists children's books and websites.

Conquistadors: Cabeza de Vaca
http://www.pbs.org/conquistadors/devaca/devaca_flat.html
The site includes video clips from the PBS television program hosted by Michael Wood, information about both Cabeza de Vaca and

Bartolomé de las Casas, and links to Conquistadors Online Learning Adventure.

The Handbook of Texas Online
http://www.tsha.utexas.edu/handbook/online
A search for "Cabeza de Vaca" will bring up a list of 126 items to explore, including information about Cabeza de Vaca and other members of the Narváez expedition, Native American groups mentioned by Cabeza de Vaca, places mentioned in the *Relación*, Texas sites he may have traveled through, the prehistory of Texas, and other early explorers of the area.

A Letter to the King of Spain by Cabeza De Vaca—An Interlinear Translation by Haniel Long
http://www.rainbowbody.net/Ongwhehonwhe/cabezalong.htm
This site makes available Haniel Long's "Interlinear to Cabeza de Vaca" (originally published in 1936), a lively condensed retelling of the *Relación* with added biographical and historical information (not all accurate) and Cabeza de Vaca's internal thoughts as imagined by Long.

New Perspectives on the West. Episode One (to 1806)
http://www.pbs.org/weta/thewest/people/a_c/cabezadevaca.htm
This site offers a brief profile of Cabeza de Vaca, the Fanny Bandelier translation of the *Relación*, and a map of his route.

Index

About the Author

Diana Childress has published four nonfiction books for young people and writes about history, archaeology, art, and literature for children's magazines and textbooks. A native of Texas, she grew up in Mexico and returned to the United States for college. Since earning her Ph.D. in medieval English literature, she has taught college English and worked as a school librarian in New York City.

Photo Acknowledgments

The images in this book are used with the permission of: The Granger Collection, New York, pp. 2, 18, 26, 30, 96; AP Photo/Texas State University, p. 8; © Visual Arts Library (London)/Alamy, p. 11; © Imagno/ Hulton Archive/Getty Images, p. 13; © North Wind Picture Archives, pp. 16, 68, 81, 108, 110; The Art Archive/Marine Museum Lisbon/Dagli Orti, p. 22; © Mary Evans Picture Library/Alamy, p. 32; © MPI/Hulton Archive/Getty Images, pp. 35, 45, 82; Courtesy of The State Archives of Florida, p. 40; Maps by Laura Westlund/Independent Picture Service, pp. 42-43, 107, 112; © Bettmann/CORBIS, pp. 48, 104; © Three Lions/ Hulton Archive/Getty Images, p. 50; © Grady Harrison/Alamy, p. 61; © Mark Zylber/Alamy, p. 65; © Bruce Dale/National Geographic/Getty Images, p. 79; Courtesy of UTSA's Institute of Texan Cultures, # 071-0243, p. 80; The Art Archive/Mireille Vautier, p. 84; © CORBIS, p. 89; © Hulton Archive/Getty Images, pp. 94, 126; © Deco Images/Alamy, p. 97; © Jason Friend/Alamy, p. 100; © The Print Collector/Alamy, p. 102; © Mary Evans Picture Library/The Image Works, p. 103; © Stapleton Collection/ CORBIS, p. 113; © Tibor Bognar/CORBIS, p. 117; © Nicole Duplaix /National Geographic/Getty Images, p. 130; Courtesy of UTSA's Institute of Texan Cultures, # 073-0926, p. 146.

Front Cover: © Jeff Greenberg/Alamy (main); © Photodisc/Getty Images (background)